THE CLAIMS OF LABOUR

The Development of Industrial Society Series

Arthur Helps

THE CLAIMS OF LABOUR

An Essay on the Duties of the
Employers to the Employed
and an Essay on
the Means of Improving the Health
and Increasing the Comfort
of the Labouring Classes

IRISH UNIVERSITY PRESS
Shannon   Ireland

First edition London 1844
Second edition London 1845

This I U P reprint is a photolithographic facsimile of
the second edition and is unabridged, retaining the
original printer's imprint.

© *1971 Irish University Press Shannon Ireland*

All forms of micropublishing
© *Irish University Microforms Shannon Ireland*

ISBN 0 7165 1598 9

T M MacGlinchey Publisher

Irish University Press Shannon Ireland

PRINTED IN THE REPUBLIC OF IRELAND BY
ROBERT HOGG PRINTER TO IRISH UNIVERSITY PRESS

The Development of Industrial Society Series

This series comprises reprints of contemporary documents and commentaries on the social, political and economic upheavals in nineteenth-century England.

England, as the first industrial nation, was also the first country to experience the tremendous social and cultural impact consequent on the alienation of people in industrialized countries from their rural ancestry. The Industrial Revolution which had begun to intensify in the mid-eighteenth century, spread swiftly from England to Europe and America. Its effects have been far-reaching: the growth of cities with their urgent social and physical problems; greater social mobility; mass education; increasingly complex administration requirements in both local and central government; the growth of democracy and the development of new theories in economics; agricultural reform and the transformation of a way of life.

While it would be pretentious to claim for a series such as this an in-depth coverage of all these aspects of the new society, the works selected range in content from *The Hungry Forties* (1904), a collection of letters by ordinary working people describing their living conditions and the effects of mechanization on their day-to-day lives, to such analytical studies as Leone Levi's *History of British Commerce* (1880) and *Wages and Earnings of the Working Classes* (1885); M. T. Sadler's *The Law of Population* (1830); John Wade's radical documentation of government corruption, *The Extraordinary Black Book* (1831); C. Edward Lester's trenchant social investigation, *The Glory and Shame of England* (1866); and many other influential books and pamphlets.

The editor's intention has been to make available important contemporary accounts, studies and records, written or compiled by men and women of integrity and scholarship whose reactions to the growth of a new kind of society are valid touchstones for today's reader. Each title (and the particular edition used) has been chosen on a twofold basis (1) its intrinsic worth as a record or commentary, and (2) its contribution to the development of an industrial society. It is hoped that this collection will help to increase our understanding of a people and an epoch.

The Editor
Irish University Press

The Claims of Labour.

AN ESSAY ON THE
DUTIES OF THE EMPLOYERS
TO THE EMPLOYED.

The Second Edition.

TO WHICH IS ADDED,

AN ESSAY ON THE MEANS OF IMPROVING THE HEALTH
AND INCREASING THE COMFORT OF THE
LABOURING CLASSES.

LONDON
WILLIAM PICKERING
1845.

" THERE is formed in every thing a double nature of good ;
" the one, as every thing is a total or substantive in itself;
" the other, as it is a part or member of a greater body;
" whereof the latter is in degree the greater and the worthier,
" because it tendeth to the conservation of a more general
" form. Therefore we see the iron in particular sympathy
" moveth to the loadstone; but yet if it exceed a certain
" quantity, it forsaketh the affection to the loadstone, and
" like a good patriot moveth to the earth, which is the re-
" gion and country of massy bodies. This double nature of
" good, and the comparative thereof, is much more engraven
" upon man, if he degenerate not; unto whom the conser-
" vation of duty to the public ought to be much more precious
" than the conservation of life and being : according to that
" memorable speech of Pompeius Magnus, when being in
" commission of purveyance for a famine at Rome, and
" being dissuaded with great vehemency and instance by his
" friends about him, that he should not hazard himself to sea
" in an extremity of weather, he said only to them, ' Ne-
" cesse est ut eam, non ut vivam.' But it may be truly
" affirmed that there was never any philosophy, religion, or
" other discipline, which did so plainly and highly exalt the
" good which is communicative, and depress the good which
" is private and particular, as the Holy Faith; well declaring,
" that it was the same God that gave the Christian law to
" men, who gave those laws of nature to inanimate crea-
" tures that we spoke of before."

Bacon's Advancement of Learning.

" AND well may masters consider how easie a transposition
" it had been for God, to have made him to mount into the
" saddle that holds the stirrup; and him to sit down at the
" table, who stands by with a trencher."

Fuller's Holy State.

TO HENRY TAYLOR, ESQ.

My dear Taylor,

I have great pleasure in dedicating this book to you, as I know of no one who, both in his life and writings, has shown a more profound and delicate care for the duties of the Employer to the Employed. Pardon me, if following the practice of the world, I see the author in his hero, and think I hear you speaking, when Van Artevelde exclaims—

> " A serviceable, faithful, thoughtful friend,
> Is old Van Ryk, and of a humble nature,
> And yet with faculties and gifts of sense,
> Which place him justly on no lowly level—
> Why should I say a lowlier than my own,
> Or otherwise than as an equal use him?
> That with familiarity respect
> Doth slacken, is a word of common use.
> I never found it so."

I have had some peculiar advantages in writing upon this subject. I should have been unobservant indeed, if, with such masters as I have served under, I had not learnt something, in regard to the duties of a great employer of labour, from witnessing their ever-flowing courtesy; their care for those who came within their sphere; their anxiety, as the heads of departments, to recognize every exertion on the part of their subordinates; and their ready sympathy with the poor and the friendless, a sympathy which the vexations and harassments of office, and all those things that tend to turn a man's thoughts in upon himself, could never subdue.

But, happily, it is not only amongst the high in office that such examples are to be found. The spirit, and even some of the very modes of benevolent exertion which I have endeavoured to recommend, have already been carried into practice, and I trust may be frequently seen, in the conduct towards their dependents, both of manufacturers and landed proprietors.

I must also say how much I owe to the excellent Reports which of late years have been presented to Parliament on subjects connected with the welfare of the labouring classes. It is to be regretted that these reports are not better known. I have made frequent use of them, and hope that the quotations I have given may induce my readers to turn to the original sources.

With regard to the subject generally, it appears to me that knowledge of the duties of an employer is every day becoming more important. The tendency of modern society is to draw the family circle within narrower and narrower limits. Those amusements which used to be shared by all classes are becoming less frequent: the great lord has put away his crowd of retainers: the farmer, in most cases, does not live with his labouring men: and the master has less sympathy and social intercourse with his domestics. If this be so, if the family circle is thus becoming narrower, the conduct of those in domestic authority, having a more intense influence, has the more need of being regulated by the highest sense of duty: and, with respect to society in general, if the old bonds are loosened, other ties must be fostered in their place.

You will not be likely to mistake my meaning, and to suppose that I look back with any fond regret at the departure of the feudal system, or that I should wish to bring the present generation under its influence. Mankind does not so retrace its steps. But still, though the course of our race is onwards, the nature of man does not change. There is the same need for protection and countenance on the one side, and for reverence and attachment on the other, that there ever has been; and the fact that society is in many respects more disconnected than it used to be, renders it the more necessary to cultivate in the most watchful manner every mode of strengthening the social intercourse between rich and poor, between master and servant, between the employers and the employed, in whatever rank they may be.

I am afraid it may be said with justice, that both this letter and the following Essay are " sermoni propiora," according to Charles Lamb's translation, " properer for a sermon:" but it is impossible to dwell long on any such subject as the one which I have chosen, without having to appeal to the best motives of human endeavour; and the shortest way even to the good which is of a purely physical character lies often, I believe, through the highest moral considerations.

Believe me,

My dear Taylor,

Most truly yours,

THE AUTHOR.

London, July 1, 1844.

THE CLAIMS OF LABOUR.

CHAPTER I.

MASTERS AND MEN.

IT is a thing so common, as almost to be ridiculous, for a man to express self-distrust at the commencement of any attempt in speech or writing. And yet, trite as this mode of beginning is, its appropriateness makes each one use it as heartily as if it were new and true for him, though it might have been a common-place for others. When he glances hurriedly across the wide extent of his subject, when he feels how inadequate his expression will be even to his conception, and, at the same time, has a yearning desire to bring his audience into the same mind with himself, it is no wonder if he begins with a few, hesitating, oft repeated, words about his own insufficiency compared with the greatness of his subject.

Happily, I have not occasion to dwell much upon the importance of the subject to which I am anxious to engage attention. For a long time it has been gradually emerging from the darkness in which it had been left. The claims of labour and the rights of the humble and the poor have necessarily gained more of the attention of mankind, as Christianity has developed itself. That power was sure, in its gradual encroachments upon the evil nature of man, to make its voice heard in this matter. It is a voice which may come out of strange bodies, such as systems of ethics, or of politics; but men may call it what they please, it goes on doing its appointed work, "conquering and to conquer."

Persons of a thoughtful mind seeing closely the falsehood, the folly, and the arrogance, of the age in which they live, are apt, occasionally, to have a great contempt for it: and I doubt not that many a man looks upon the present time as one of feebleness and degeneracy. There are, however, signs of an increased solicitude for the claims of labour, which of itself is a thing of the highest promise, and more to be rejoiced over than all the mechanical triumphs which both those who would magnify, and those who would depreciate, the present age, would be apt to point to as containing its especial significance and merit.

But what do all these mechanical triumphs come to? It is in vain that you have learned to move with double or treble the velocity of your immediate predecessors: it is in vain that you can show new modes of luxury, or new resources in art. The inquiring historian will give these things their weight, but will, nevertheless, persevere in asking how the great mass of the people were fed, and clothed, and taught: and whether the improvement in their condition corresponded at all with the improvement of the condition of the middle and upper classes. What a sorry answer any one, replying for this age, would have to give him. Nor would it be enough, indeed, if we could make a satisfactory reply to his questions about the physical state of the people. We ought to be able to say that the different orders of society were bound together by links of gratitude and regard : that they were not like layers of various coloured sand, but that they formed one solid whole of masonry, each part having its relation of use and beauty to all the others.

Certainly, if we look at the matter, we have not much to say for ourselves, unless it be in that dawning of good intentions which I have alluded to before. There is to be found in our metropolis, in our great towns, and even in our rural districts, an extent of squalid misery such as we are almost afraid to give heed to, and which we are glad to forget as soon as we have read or heard of it. It may be that our ancestors endured, it may be that many savage tribes still endure, far more privation than is to be found in the sufferings of our lowest class. But the mind refuses to consider the two states as analogous, and insists upon thinking that the state of physical and moral degradation often found amongst our working classes, with the arabesque of splendour and luxury which surrounds it, is a more shocking thing to contemplate than a pressing scarcity of provisions endured by a wandering horde of savage men sunk in equal barbarism. When we follow men home, who have been cooperating with other civilized men in continuous labour throughout the livelong day, we should not, without experience, expect to find their homes dreary, comfortless, deformed with filth, such homes as poverty alone could not make. Still less, when we gaze upon some pleasant looking village, fair enough in outward seeming for poets' songs to celebrate, should we expect to find scarcity of fuel, scantiness of food, prevalence of fever, the healthy huddled together with the sick, decency outraged, and self-respect all gone. And yet such sights, both in town and country, if not of habitual occurrence, are at any rate sadly too numerous for us to pass them by as rare and exceptional cases.

Is this then the inevitable nature of things? Has the boasted civilization of the world led only to this? Do we master the powers of nature only to let forth a new and fierce torrent of social miseries upon us? Let not such thoughts be ours. Pagans, the slaves of destiny, might well have held them. But we cannot doubt that the conditions of labour, under which man holds the earth, express the mercy and the goodness, no less than the judgment, of God.

Many benevolent persons feel, doubtless, very sensitively for the sad condition of the labouring classes, and are anxiously looking about for remedies to meet it. I would not speak slightingly of any attempt in that direction. There are problems in political economy, in government, and, perhaps, even in the adaptation of machinery, which may be worked out with signal service to the great cause of suffering humanity. It is not my intention, however, to dwell upon such topics. My object is to show what can be done with the means that are at the present moment in every body's power. Many a man, who is looking about for some specific, has in his hands the immediate means of doing great good, which he would be ready enough to employ, if he had but imagination to perceive that he possessed them. My endeavour then will simply be to show what can be

done by the employers of labour in their individual and private capacity.

What an important relation is that of Master and Man !   How it pervades the world ;
ascending from the lowest gradation of planter
and slave through the states of master and
servant, landlord and labourer, manufacturer
and artisan, till it comes to the higher degrees
of rule which one cultivated man has to exercise over another in the performance of the
greatest functions.   See, throughout, what
difficulties and temptations encumber this
relation.   How boundless is the field of
thought which it opens to us, how infinite the
duties which it contains, how complete an
exercise it is for the whole faculties of man.
Observe what wretchedness is caused by a
misunderstanding of this relation in domestic
matters.   See the selfish carelessness about
the happiness of those around them of men
not ill-intentioned, nor unkind, perhaps, in
their dealings with the world in general, but
lamentably unfit for the management of a
home.   Then observe the effects of similar

mismanagement in dealing with a country.
Look at the listless loiterers about an Irish
town : you would naturally say to yourself,
" Surely this people have done all that there
can be for them to do." You walk out of
the town, and find the adjacent fields as
listless-looking, and neglected, as the men
themselves. Think what a want there must
be of masters of labour, that those hands
and these weeds are not brought into closer
contact.

It may be said that the distressed condition of the labouring classes is owing to tem-
porary causes, and that good times, by which
is meant good wages, would remove a large
part of the evil. I confess it does not appear
to me that a good harvest or two, or ready
customers on the other side of the Atlantic,
or the home demand that may arise from
exhausted stocks, or any other cause of that
nature which is simply to end in better wages,
would of itself do all, or even any considerable part, of what we should desire. I do not,
for a moment, mean·to depreciate the good
effects that would flow from an increase of

employment and better wages. But still I
imagine that there are many cases in which,
if you were, in ordinary times, to double the
amount of wages, a very inadequate proportion of good would follow. You have to teach
these poor people how to spend money: you
have to give them the opportunities of doing
so to advantage: you have to provide a system of education which shall not vary with
every fluctuation of trade: and to adopt such
methods of working as shall make the least
possible disturbance of domestic ties. No
sudden influx of money will do all these
things. In fact, whatever part of this subject one takes up, one is perpetually brought
back to the conviction of the necessity which
exists for an earnest and practical application, on the part of the employing class, of
thought and labour for the welfare of those
whom they employ.

Some of my readers may think that I have
spoken of the distress of the labouring population in exaggerated terms. Let them only
read the details of it in the Report of 1842,
on the Sanitary Condition of the labouring

population, or in the Report of last year, on
the condition of the children and young persons employed in mines and manufactures.
I scarcely know what extracts to give of these
direful reports, that may briefly convey the
state of things to those who have not studied
the subject. Shall I tell them of children
ignorant who Jesus Christ was ; or of others
who know no more of the Lord's Prayer
than the first words, " Our Father :" and
whose nightly prayers begin and end with
those two words ? Shall I tell them of great
towns in which one half at least of the juvenile population is growing up without education of any kind whatever? Shall I show that
working people are often permitted to pass
their labour time, the half of their lives, in
mines, workshops, and manufactories, where
an atmosphere of a deleterious kind prevails :
and this, too, not from any invincible evil in
the nature of the employment, but from a
careless or penurious neglect on the part of
their employers? Shall I go into a lengthened description of the habitations of the
poor which will show that they are often
worse housed than beasts of burden? Or

need I depict at large the dark stream of profligacy which overflows and burns into those parts of the land where such Want and Ignorance prevail?

How many of these evils might have been mitigated, if not fully removed, had each generation of masters done but a small part of its duty in the way of amelioration. But it was not of such things that they were thinking. The thoughtless cruelty in the world almost outweighs the rest.

"Why vex me with these things?" exclaims the general reader. "Have we not enough " of dismal stories? It oppresses us to hear " them. Let us hope that something will " occur to prevent such things in future. " But I am not a redresser of grievances. " Let those who live by the manufacturing " system cure the evils incident to it. Oh " that there had never been such a thing as " a manufacturing system!" With thoughts vague, recriminatory, and despondent, as the foregoing, does many a man push from him all consideration on the subject. It is so easy to despair: and the largeness of a calamity is so ready a shelter for those who

have not heart enough to adventure any opposition to it.

Thus, by dwelling upon the magnitude of
the evils we long to lessen, we are frightened
and soothed into letting our benevolent wishes
remain as wishes only. But surely a man
may find a sphere small enough, as well as
large enough, for him to act in. In all other
pursuits, we are obliged to limit the number
and extent of our objects, in order to give full
effect to our endeavours: and so it should
be with benevolence. The foolish sluggard
stares hopelessly into the intricacies of the
forest, and thinks that it can never be re-
claimed. The wiser man, the labourer, begins
at his corner of the wood, and makes out a
task for himself for each day. Let not our
imaginations be employed on one side only.
Think, that large as may appear the work to
be done—so too the result of any endeavour,
however small in itself, may be of infinite
extent in the future. Nothing is lost.

And why should we despair? A great
nation is never in extreme peril until it has
lost its hopeful spirit. If, at this moment, a

foreign enemy were on the point of invading
us, how strenuous we should be : what moral
energy would instantly pervade us. Faster
than the beacon lights could give the intelli-
gence from headland to headland ; from city
to city would spread the national enthusiasm
of a people that would never admit the
thought of being conquered. Trust me, these
domestic evils are foes not less worthy of our
attention than any foreign invaders. It seems
to me, I must confess, a thing far more to be
dreaded, that any considerable part of our
population should be growing up in a state
of absolute ignorance, than would be the
danger, not new to us, of the combined hostility of the civilized world. Our trials, as a
nation, like our individual ones, are perpetually varied as the world progresses.

> " The old order changeth, yielding place to new,
>   And God fulfils himself in many ways."

We have not the same evils to contend with
as our ancestors had ; but we need the same
stoutness of heart that bore them through
the contest. The sudden growth of things,
excellent in themselves, entangles the feet of

that generation amongst whom they spring
up. There may be something, too, in the
progress of human affairs like the coming in
of the tide, which, for each succeeding wave,
often seems as much of a retreat as an ad-
vance : but still the tide comes on.

The settled state of things attendant upon
peace, and an unquestioned dynasty, is good,
as it enables men to look more to civil affairs ;
but it has, perhaps, a drawback in a certain
apathy which is wont to accompany it. The
ordinary arrangements of social life, for a
long time uninterrupted by any large calamity, appear to become hardened into cer-
tainties. A similar course of argument would,
on a large scale, apply not only to this
country, but to the world in general. Security is the chief end of civilization, and as it
progresses, the fortunes of individuals are,
upon the whole, made less liable to derange-
ment. This very security may tend to make
men careless of the welfare of others, and, as
Bacon would express it, may be noted as an
impediment to benevolence. I have often
thought, whether in former times, when men

looked to those immediately around them as
their body guard against sudden and violent
attacks, they ventured to show as much ill-
temper to those they lived with as you sometimes see them do now, when assistance of all
kinds is a purchasable commodity. Considerations of this nature are particularly applicable when addressed to persons living in a
great capital like London. All things that
concern the nation, its joys, its sorrows, and
its successes, are transacted in this metropolis; or, as one might more properly say,
are represented in transactions in this metropolis. But still this often happens in such a
manner as would be imperceptible even to
people of vast experience and observation.
The countless impulses which travel up from
various directions to this absorbing centre
sometimes neutralize each other, and leave a
comparative calm ; or they create so complex
an agitation, that it may be next to impossible for us to discern and estimate the component forces. Hence the metropolis may
not at times be sufficiently susceptible in the
case either of manufacturing or agricultural
distress, or of any colonial perturbation. This

metropolitan insensibility has some great advantages, but it is well for us to observe the
corresponding evil, and, as far as may be, to
guard our own hearts from being rendered
apathetic by its influence.

I do not seek to terrify any one into a
care for the labouring classes, by representing
the danger to society of neglecting them. It
is certainly a fearful thing to think of large
masses of men being in that state of want
and misery which leaves them nothing to
hazard; and who are likely to be without
the slightest reverence or love for the institutions around them. Still it is not to any
fear, grounded on such considerations, that I
would appeal. The flood-gates may be strong
enough to keep out the torrent for our time.
These things are not in our reckonings. Occasionally the upheaving of the waves may
frighten timid, selfish, men into concessions
which they would not otherwise have made;
but those whom I would seek to influence,
are likely to court danger and difficulty rather
than to shun it. Nor would I even care to
disturb the purely selfish man by dwelling
studiously on any social dangers around us,

or labouring to discern in present disturbance
or distress the seeds of inevitable revolution.
No, I would say to him, if it all ends here,

" But here, upon this bank and shoal of time,"

you may have chosen wisely. It is true,
there are sources of happiness which you
now know nothing of, and which may be far
beyond any selfish gratification you have ever
experienced. Indeed, it may be, that you
cannot enjoy the highest delights without
sharing them, that they are not things to be
given out to each of us as individuals, now
to this man, then to that, but that they require a community of love. But, at any rate,
I do not wish to scare you into active and
useful exertion by indicating that you are,
otherwise, in danger of losing any of the
good things of this world.

The great motive to appeal to, is not a
man's apprehension of personal loss or suffering, but his fear of neglecting a sacred
duty. And it will be found here, I believe,
as elsewhere, that the highest motives are
those of the most sustained efficiency.

But little as I would counsel despair, or

encourage apathy, or seek to influence by
terror, it is not that I look to the " course
of events," or any other rounded collection
of words, to do anything for us. What is
this " course of events" but the continuity
of human endeavour ? And giving all due
weight to the influence of those general currents which attend the progress of opinions
and institutions, we must still allow largely
for the effect of individual character, and individual exertions. The main direction that
the stream will take is manifest enough perhaps ; but it may come down upon long tracts
of level ground which it will overspread
quietly, or it may enter into some rocky
channel which will control it ; or it may meet
with some ineffectual mud embankment which
it will overthrow with devastation.

Putting aside then such phrases as " course
of events," and the like, let us look to men.
And whom shall we look to first but the
Masters of Thought ? Surely the true poet
will do something to lift the burden of his
own age. What is the use of wondrous gifts
of language, if they are employed to enervate,

and not to ennoble, their hearers? What avails it to trim the lights of history, if they are made to throw no brightness on the present, or open no track into the future? And to employ Imagination only in the service of Vanity, or Gain, is as if an astronomer were to use his telescope to magnify the potherbs in his kitchen garden.

Think what a glorious power is that of expression: and what responsibility follows the man who possesses it. That grace of language which can make even commonplace things beautiful, throwing robes of the poorest texture into forms of all-attractive loveliness: why does it not expend its genius on materials that would be worthy of the artist? The great interests of Man are before it, are crying for it, can absorb all its endeavour, are, indeed, the noblest field for it. Think of this—then think what a waste of high intellectual endowments there has been in all ages from the meanest of motives. But what wise man would not rather have the harmless fame, which youths, on a holiday, scratch for themselves upon the leaden roof of some cathedral tower, than enjoy the unde-

niable renown of those who, with whatever
power, have written from slight or unworthy
motives what may prove a hindrance, rather
than an aid, to the well-being of their fellow-
men ?

But, passing from those who are often the
real, though unrecognized, rulers of their
own age, and the despots of the succeeding
generation, let us turn to the ostensible and
immediate ruling powers.   Assuredly the
government may do something towards removing part of the evils we have been considering as connected with the system of
labour.   It seems as if there were a want of
more departments; and certainly of many
more able men.   The progress of any social
improvement appears to depend too much on
chance and clamour.   I do not suppose, for a
moment, that we can have the cut-and-dried
executive, or legislative, arrangements that
belong to despotic governments; and it is, in
some respects, a wholesome fear that we have
of the interference of government.   Still, we
may recollect that England is not a small

state, nor an inactive one, where the public
energies are likely to be deadened, or over-
ridden, by activity on the part of the government, which might, perhaps, with much safety
undertake more than it has been wont to do.
One thing is certain, that it may do great
good, if it would but look out for men of
ability to fill the offices at present in its gift.
No government need fear such a course as
destructive to its party interests. In appoint-
ing and promoting the fittest men, you are
likely to ensure more gratitude than if you
selected those, who being the creatures of
your kindness, could never, you imagine, be
otherwise than most grateful for it. Weak
people are seldom much given to gratitude:
and even if they were, it is dearly that you
purchase their allegiance; for there are few
things which, on the long run, displease the
public more than bad appointments. But,
putting aside the political expediency either
way, it is really a sacred duty in a statesman
to choose fit agents. Observe the whirlpool
of folly that a weak man contrives to create
round him : and see, on the other hand, with

what small means, a wise man manages to have influence and respect, and force, in whatever may be his sphere.

I have thought, for example, with regard to the Suppression of the Slave Trade, that amongst all the devices that can be suggested, one of the first things would be to tempt very superior men, by large inducements, to take the judicial situations in the Mixed Commissions, or any other appointments, in slave-trading parts of the world. We may expect great results whenever real ability is brought into personal contact with the evils we wish it to overcome.

There is a matter connected with the functions of government which seems to be worthy of notice; and that is, the distribution of honours. These honours are part of the resources of the state; and it is a most spendthrift thing to bestow them as they frequently are bestowed. It is not merely that government gives them unworthily: it absolutely plays with them; gives them, as one might say, for the drollery of the thing, when it adds a title to some foolish person, whose merits not even the Public Orator at a uni-

versity could discover. It is idle to talk of
such things being customary. A great minister would not recommend his sovereign to
confer honours on such people; and sensible
men would be glad to see that the resources
of the state, in all ways, were dealt with con-
siderately.

The above reflections are not foreign to
the main subject of this essay; for a government, having at heart the improvement of
the labouring population, or any other social
matter, might direct the stream of honours
towards those who were of service to the state
in this matter, and so might make the civic
crown what it was in ancient days. Not,
however, that I mean to say that the best
men are to be swayed by these baubles. The
hope of reward is not the source of the highest
endeavour.

There is a class of persons who interest
themselves so far in the condition of the
labouring population, as to bring forward
sad instances of suffering, and then to say,
" Our rich men should look to these things."
This kind of benevolence delights to bring

together, in startling contrast, the condition of different classes, and then to indulge in much moral reflection. Now riches are very potent in their way; but a great heart is often more wanted than a full purse. I speak it not in any disparagement of the rich or great, when I say that we must not trust to them alone. Amongst them are many who use their riches as God's stewards; but the evils which we have to contend against are to be met by a general impulse in the right direction of people of all classes. There are instances where a man's wealth enables him to set forth more distinctly to the world's eye some work of benevolence, even to be the pioneer in improvements, which persons of smaller fortunes could scarcely have effected. In such a case great indeed is the advantage of riches. But do not let us accustom our minds to throw the burden of good works on the shoulders of any particular class. God has not given a monopoly of benevolence to the rich.

What I have just said about individual rich men, applies in some measure to associations for benevolent purposes. They are to be looked upon as accessories—sometimes very useful ones—but they are not to be expected to supersede private enterprise. A man should neither wait for them; nor, when they exist, should he try to throw his duties upon them, and indolently expect that they are to think and act in all cases for him. Wherever a strong feeling on any subject exists, societies will naturally spring up in connexion with it. What such bodies have to do, is to direct their energies to those parts of the matter in which it is especially difficult for private enterprise to succeed. And private individuals should be cautious of slackening their endeavours in any good cause, merely because they are aware that some society exists which has the same object in view.

I come now to some member of that large class of persons who are not rich, nor great employers of labour, nor in any station of peculiar influence. He shudders as he reads those startling instances of suffering or crime in which the distress and ignorance of the labouring population will, occasionally, break

out into the notice of the world. "What can
I do?" he exclaims. "I feel with intensity
the horrors I read of: but what can one man
do?" I only ask him to study what he feels.
He is a citizen. He cannot be such an isolated being as to have no influence. The
conclusions which he comes to, after mature
reflection, will not be without their weight.
If individual citizens were anxious to form
their opinions with care, on those questions
respecting which they will have to vote and
to act, there would be little need of organized
bodies of men to carry great measures into
effect. The main current of public opinion
is made up of innumerable rills, so small,
perhaps, that a child might with its foot
divert the course of any one of them: but
collected together they rush down with a
force that is irresistible. If those who have
actively to distribute the labour of the world
knew that you, the great mass of private
men, regarded them not for their money, but
for their conduct to those in their employ,
not for the portion which they may contrive
to get for themselves, but for the well-being
which they may give rise to, and regulate

amongst others; why then your thoughts
would be motives to them, urging them on in
the right path. Besides, you would not stop
at thinking. The man who gives time and
thought to the welfare of others will seldom
be found to grudge them anything else.

Again, have not you, though not manufacturers, or master-workmen, or owners of
land, have not you dependents, in whose be-
half you may find exercise for the principles
to which I am convinced that study in this
matter will lead you? Your regard for servants is a case in point. And, moreover, you
may show in your ordinary, every day, dealings with the employers of labour a consi-
derateness for those under them, which may
awaken the employers to a more lively care
themselves. Only reflect on the duty: opportunities of testing the strength of your
resolves will not be wanting.

We sometimes feel thoroughly impressed
by some good thought, or just example, that
we meet with in study or real life, but as if
we had no means of applying it. We cannot
at once shape for ourselves a course that
shall embrace this newly acquired wisdom.

Often it seems too grand for the occasions of ordinary life; and we fear that we must keep it laid up for some eventful day, as nice housewives their stateliest furniture. However, if we keep it close to the heart, and make but the least beginning with it, our infant practice leads to something better, or grows into something ampler. In real life there are no isolated points.

You, who have but few dependents, or, perhaps, but one drudge dependent upon you, whether as servant, apprentice, or hired labourer, do not think that you have not an ample opportunity for exercising the duties of an employer of labour. Do not suppose that these duties belong to the great manufacturer with the population of a small town in his own factory, or to the landlord with vast territorial possessions, and that you have nothing to do with them. The Searcher of all hearts may make as ample a trial of you in your conduct to one poor dependent, as of the man who is appointed to lead armies and administer provinces. Nay, your treatment of some animal entrusted to your care may be a history as significant for you, as the chronicles of kings for them. The moral experiments in the world may be tried with the smallest quantities.

I cannot quit this part of the subject without alluding more directly to the duties of the employers of domestic servants. Of course the principles which should regulate the conduct of masters and mistresses towards their servants, are the same as those which should regulate the employers of labour generally. But there are some peculiar circumstances which need to be noticed in the application of these principles. That, in this case, the employers and the employed are members of one family, is a circumstance which intensifies the relation. It is a sad thing for a man to pass the working part of his day with an exacting, unkind, master: but still, if the workman returns at evening to a home that is his own, there is a sense of coming joy and freedom which may support him throughout the weary hours of labour. But think what it must be to share one's home with one's oppressor; to have no recurring time when one is certain to be free from those harsh words, and unjust censures, which are almost more than blows, aye even to those natures we are apt to fancy so hardened to rebuke. Imagine the deadness of heart that must prevail in that poor wretch who never hears the sweet words of praise or of encouragement. Many masters of families, men living in the rapid current of the world, who are subject to a variety of impressions which, in their busy minds, are made and effaced even in the course of a single day, can with difficulty estimate the force of unkind words upon those whose monotonous life leaves few opportunities of effacing any unwelcome impression. There is nothing in which the aid of imagination, that handmaid of charity, may be more advantageously employed, than in considering the condition of domestic servants. Let a man endeavour to realize it to himself, let him think of its narrow sphere, of its unvarying nature, and he will be careful not to throw in, unnecessarily, the trouble even of a single harsh word, which may make so large a disturbance in the shallow current of a domestic's hopes and joys. How often, on the contrary, do you find that

masters seem to have no apprehension of the
feelings of those under them, no idea of any
duties on their side beyond " cash payment,"
whereas the good, old, patriarchal feeling towards your household is one which the mere
introduction of money wages has not by any
means superseded, and which cannot, in fact,
be superseded.   You would bear with lenity
from a child many things, for which, in a
servant, you can find nothing but the harshest
names.   Yet how often are these poor, uneducated, creatures little better than children!   You talk, too, of ingratitude from
them, when, if you reflected a little, you
would see that they do not understand your
benefits.   It is hard enough sometimes to
make benefits sink into men's hearts, even
when your good offices are illustrated by
much kindness of words and manner; but to
expect that servants should at once appreciate your care for them is surely most unreasonable, especially if it is not accompanied
by a manifest regard and sympathy.   You
would not expect it, if you saw the child-like
relation in which they stand to you.

Another mode of viewing with charity the

conduct of domestic servants, is to imagine
what manner of servant you would make yourself, or any one of those whom in your own
rank you esteem and love.   Do you not perceive, in almost every character, some element which would occasionally make its pos-
sessor fail in performing the duties of domestic service? Do you find that faithfulness,
accuracy, diligence, and truth pervade the
circle of your equals in such abundance that
you should be exorbitantly angry, the moment you perceive a deficiency in such qualities amongst those who have been but indif-
ferently brought up, and who, perhaps, have
early imbibed those vices of their class, fear
and falsehood; vices which their employers
can only hope to eradicate by a long course
of considerate kindness?

I do not speak of the conduct of masters
and mistresses as an easy matter : on the
contrary, I believe that it is one of the most
difficult functions in life. If, however, men
only saw the difficulty, they would see the
worthiness of trying to overcome it. You
observe a man becoming day by day richer,

or advancing in station, or increasing in professional reputation, and you set him down as a successful man in life. But, if his home is an ill-regulated one, where no links of affection extend throughout the family, whose former domestics (and he has had more of them than he can well remember) look back upon their sojourn with him as one unblessed by kind words or deeds, I contend that that man has not been successful. Whatever good fortune he may have in the world, it is to be remembered that he has always left one important fortress untaken behind him. That man's life does not surely read well whose benevolence has found no central home. It may have sent forth rays in various directions, but there should have been a warm focus of love—that home nest which is formed round a good man's heart.

Having spoken of some of the duties of private persons, we come now to the great employers of labour. Would that they all saw the greatness of their position. Strange as it may sound, they are the successors of the feudal barons, they it is who lead thousands to peaceful conquests, and upon whom, in great measure, depends the happiness of large masses of mankind. As Mr. Carlyle says, " The Leaders of Industry, if Industry is ever " to be led, are virtually the Captains of the " World ; if there be no nobleness in them, " there will never be an Aristocracy more." Can a man, who has this destiny entrusted to him, imagine that his vocation consists merely in getting together a large lump of gold, and then being off with it, to enjoy it, as he fancies, in some other place : as if that which is but a small part of his business in life, were all in all to him ; as if indeed, the parable of the talents were to be taken literally, and that a man should think that he has done his part when he has made much gold and silver out of little ? If these men saw their position rightly, what would be their objects, what their pleasures ? Their objects would not consist in foolish vyings with each other about the grandeur or the glitter of life. But in directing the employment of labour, they would find room for the exercise of all the powers of their minds, of their best affections, and of whatever was worthy in their ambition.

Their occupation, so far from being a limited
sphere of action, is one which may give scope
to minds of the most various capacity. While
one man may undertake those obvious labours
of benevolent superintendence which are of
immediate and pressing necessity, another
may devote himself to more remote and indirect methods of improving the condition of
those about him, which are often not the
less valuable because of their indirectness.
In short, it is evident that to lead the labour
of large masses of people, and to do that, not
merely with a view to the greatest product
of commodities, but to the best interests of
the producers, is a matter which will sufficiently and worthily occupy men of the
strongest minds aided by all the attainments
which cultivation can bestow.

I do not wish to assert a principle larger
than the occasion demands : and I am, therefore unwilling to declare that we cannot justly
enter into a relation so meagre with our fel-
low-creatures, as that of employing all their
labour, and giving them nothing but money in
return. There might, perhaps, be a state of
society in which such a relation would not be

culpable, a state in which the great mass of the employed were cultivated and considerate men; and where the common interests of master and man were well understood. But we have not to deal with any such imaginary case. So far from working men being the considerate creatures we have just imagined them, it is absolutely requisite to protect, in the most stringent manner, the interests of the children against the parents, who are often anxious to employ their little ones most immaturely. Nay more—it is notorious that working men will frequently omit to take even the slightest precaution in matters connected with the preservation of their own lives. If these poor men do not demand from you as Christians something more than mere money wages, what do the injunctions about charity mean? If those employed by you are not your neighbours, who are?

But, some great employer may exclaim: " It is hard that we the agents between the consumer and the producer should have all the sacrifices to make, should have all the labouring population thrown, as it were, on

our hands." In reply, I say that I have laid
down no such doctrine. I have urged the
consumer to perform his duties, and tried to
point out to him what some of those duties
are. As a citizen, he may employ himself in
understanding this subject, and in directing
others rightly; he may, in his capacity of
voter, or in his fair influence on voters, urge
upon the state its duty, and show, that as an
individual, he would gladly bear his share of
any increased burdens which that duty might
entail upon the state. He may prove in
many ways, as a mere purchaser, his concern
for the interests of the producer. And there
are, doubtless, occasions on which you, the
great employers of labour, may call upon him
to make large sacrifices of his money, his
time, and his thoughts, for the welfare of the
labouring classes. His example and his encouragement may cheer you on; and as a
citizen, as an instructor, as a neighbour, in
all the capacities of life, he may act and speak
in a way that may indirectly, if not directly,
support your more manifest endeavours in the
same good cause. It is to no one class that
I speak. We are all bound to do something

towards this good work. If, hereafter, I go
more into detail as regards the especial methods of improving his work-people that a
manufacturer might employ, it is not that I
wish to point out manufacturers as a class
especially deficient in right feelings towards
those under them. Far from it. Much of
what I shall venture to suggest has been
learnt from what I have seen and heard,
amongst the manufacturers themselves.

CHAPTER II.

SOCIAL GOVERNMENT.

SUPPOSING, reader, that whether you are manufacturer, master-workman, owner of land, or private individual, you are now thoroughly impressed with the duty of attending to the welfare of your dependants; I proceed to make some general reflections which may aid you in your outset, or sustain you in the progress, of your endeavours.

And, first, let me implore you not to delay that outset. Make a beginning at once, at least in investigating the matters to which I have striven to draw your attention. It is no curious work of art that you have to take up; it requires no nicety of apprehension;

you can hardly begin wrongly, I do not say
in action, but in the preparation for action.
However little of each day you may be able
to call your own for this purpose, it is better
to begin with that little than to wait for some
signal time of leisure. Routine encumbers
us; our days are frittered away by most
minute employments that we cannot control;
and, when spare moments do occur, we are
mostly unprepared with any pursuits of our
own to go on with. Hence it is, that the
most obvious evils go on, generation after
generation, people not having time, as they
would say, to interfere. Men are for ever
putting off the concerns which should be
dearest to them to a " more convenient season," when, as they hope, there may be
fewer trifles to distract their attention: but
a great work, which is to commence in the
heart, requires not to have the first stone laid
for it, with pomp, upon some holiday. It is
good to have made a beginning upon it at
any time.

The wisdom, or the folly, of delay is in
most instances like that of a traveller coming
to a stream, and wishing to ford it, yet con-

tinuing his journey along its banks : and whether this is wise, or not, depends mainly on
the simple fact, of whether he is walking up
to the source, or down to the fall. The latter
is apt to be the direction in the case of our
generous resolves : their difficulty widens as
we delay to act upon them.

Throughout the progress of your work,
there is nothing that you will have more frequently to be mindful of than your views with
respect to self-advancement. To take one
form of it, the acquisition of money. Money,
as Charles Lamb, a great despiser of cant,
observed, is not dross, but books, pictures,
wines, and many pleasant things. Still I
suspect that money is more sought after to
gratify vanity, than to possess the means of
enjoying any of the above named pleasant
things. Money is so much desired, because
it is a measure of success; so much regretted,
because we fancy the loss of it leaves us
powerless and contemptible. That kind of
satire, therefore, which delights to dwell upon
the general subserviency to wealth is not
likely to make men less desirous of riches.

But a man would be likely to estimate more reasonably the possession of money and of all kinds of self-advancement, if he did but perceive, that even a man's worldly success is not to be measured by his success for himself alone, but by the result of his endeavours for the great family of man.

There is a source of contemplation which nature affords us, one, too, that is open to the dweller in crowded cities as well as to the shepherd on Salisbury plain, and which might sometimes suggest the foolishness of an inordinate love of money. Consider the prospect which each unveiled night affords us, telling of wonders such as we have hardly the units of measurement to estimate; and then think how strange it is that we should ever allow our petty personal possessions of to-day to render us blind to the duties, which, alone, are the great realities of life. There was some excuse, perhaps, for the men of olden time, who looked upon this earth, the birth-place of their gods, as no mean territory. That they should dote upon terrestrial things was not to be wondered at. But what is to be said for us who know that this small planet is but a speck, as it were, from which we look out upon the profusion of immensity. To think that a man, who knows this, should nevertheless not hesitate to soil his soul, lying here, cringing there, pursuing tortuous schemes of most corrupt policy; or that he should ever suffer himself to be immersed, innocently, if it may be so, in selfish, worldly pursuits, forgetful of all else; when, at the best, it is but to win some acres of this transitory earth, or to be noted as one who has been successful for himself. The folly of the gambling savage, who stakes his liberty against a handful of cowrie shells is nothing to it.

Perhaps the next thing that is likely to divert you from useful endeavours for the benefit of others is fear of criticism: you do not know what the world will say: indeed, they may pronounce you an enthusiast, which word, of itself, is an icy blast of ridicule to a timid mind. You shudder at doing anything unusual, and even hear by anticipation the laugh of your particular friends. You are especially ashamed at appearing to care for

what those about you do not care for. A
laugh at your humanity, or your " theories,"
would disconcert you. You are fearfully
anxious that any project of benevolence you
undertake should succeed, not altogether on
its own account, but because your sagacity
is embarked in it, and plentiful will be the
gibes at its failure, if it should fail. Put
these fears aside. All that is prominent, all
that acts, must lay itself open to shallow criticism. It has been said that in no case of
old age, however extreme, has the faculty
for giving advice been known to decay ; depend upon it, that of criticism flourishes in
the most indolent, the most feeble, the most
doting minds. Let not the wheels of your
endeavour be stayed by accumulated rubbish
of this kind. We are afraid of responsibility,
afraid of what people may say of us, afraid of
being alone in doing right: in short, the courage which is allied to no passion—Christian
courage as it may be called—is in all ages
and amongst all people, one of the rarest
possessions.

The fear of ridicule is the effeminacy of the
soul.

Great enterprises—and for you this attempt to make your working men happier is a great enterprise—great enterprises demand an habitual self-sacrifice in little things : and, hard as it may be to keep fully in mind the enterprise itself, it is often harder still to maintain a just sense of the connection between it and these said trifling points of conduct, which, perhaps, in any single instance, seem so slightly and so remotely connected with it. But remember it is not always over great impediments that men are liable to stumble most fatally.

You must not expect immediate and obvious gratitude to crown your exertions. The benevolence that has not duty for its stem, but merely springs from some affectionateness of nature, must often languish, I fear, when it comes to count up its returns in the way of grateful affection from those whom it has toiled for. And yet the fault is often as much in the impatience and unreasonable expectation of the benefactors, as in any ingratitude on the part of the persons benefited.

If you must look for gratitude, at any rate consider whether your exertions are likely to be fully understood at present by those whom you have served; and whether it is not a reversion, rather than an immediate return, that you should look for—a reversion, too, in many cases to be realized only on the death of the benefactor. Moreover, it is useless and unreasonable to expect that any motives of gratitude will uniformly modify for you the peculiar tempers and dispositions of those whom you have served. Your benefits did not represent a permanent state of mind: neither will their gratitude. The sense of obligation, even in most faithful hearts, is often dormant; but evil tempers answer quickly to the lightest summons.

In all your projects for the good of others, beware lest your benevolence should have too much of a spirit of interference. Consider what it is you want to produce. Not an outward, passive, conformity to your wishes, but something vital which shall generate the feelings and habits you long to see manifested. You can clip a tree into

any form you please, but if you wish it to
bear fruit when it has been barren, you must
attend to what is beneath the surface, you
must feed the roots. You must furnish it
with that nutriment, you must supply it with
those opportunities of sunshine, which will
enable it to use its own energies. See how
the general course of the world is governed.
How slowly are those great improvements
matured which our impatient nature might
expect to have been effected at a single stroke.
What tyrannies have been under the sun,
things which we can hardly read of without
longing for some direct divine interference to
have taken place. Indeed, if other testimony
were wanting, the cruelties permitted on
earth present an awful idea of the general
freedom of action entrusted to mankind. And
can you think that it is left for you to drill
men suddenly into your notions, or to produce moral ends by mere mechanical means?
You will avoid much of this foolish spirit if
you are really unselfish in your purposes; if,
in dealing with those whom you would benefit, you refer your operations to them as
the centre, and not to yourself, and the suc-

cesses of your plans. There is a noble passage
in the history of the first great Douglas, the
" good Lord James," who, just before the
battle of Bannockburn, seeing Randolph, his
rival in arms, with a small body of men,
contending against a much superior English
force, rushed to his aid. " The little body
" of Randolph," says Sir Walter Scott, " was
" seen emerging like a rock in the waves, from
" which the English cavalry were retreating
" on every side with broken ranks, like a
" repelled tide. ' Hold and halt !' said the
" Douglas to his followers ; 'we are come too
" late to aid them ; let us not lessen the vic-
" tory they have won by affecting to claim a
" share in it.' " It is the self-denying nature
of this chivalrous deed that I would apply
to far other circumstances. The interfering
spirit, which I deprecate, would come, not
to consummate the victory, but to hinder it.

For similar reasons I would have you take
care that you do not adopt mere rules, and
seek to impress them rigidly upon others, as
if they were general principles, which must
at once be suitable to all mankind. Do not
imagine that your individual threads of ex-

perience form a woven garment of prudence, capable of fitting with exactness any member of the whole human family.

There are several ungenerous motives, of some subtlety, which hide in the dark corners of the heart, and stand in the way of benevolence. For instance, even in good minds, there is apt to lurk some tinge of fear, or of dislike, at the prospect of an undoubted amelioration of the lot of others coming too fast, as these good people would say. Indeed, some persons find it hard to reconcile themselves to the idea of others' burdens being readily removed, even when they themselves are making exertions to remove them.

Another feeling to beware of, is that of envy, which, strange as it seems, may sometimes arise upon the view of that very prosperity, which the person, feeling envy, has helped to create. The truth is, it is comparatively easy to avoid being envious of the good fortune which was established before our time, or which is out of our own sphere: but to be quite pleased with the good fortune of those whom we recollect in other circumstances, and who, perhaps, have been accustomed to ask advice or assistance from us—that is the trial.

Another ungenerous sentiment, similar to the foregoing, and likely at times to prove a hindrance to benevolent exertion, arises from the comparison of our own past lot with that of the persons whose condition is sought to be improved. Most of us have a little tendency to grudge them this amelioration. We should shudder at the brutality of one, who, having attained to power, is more cruel because he has suffered much himself, ("*eo immitior quia toleraverat*"); but are we not of a like spirit, if any dissatisfaction steals over our minds at seeing others exempt from those sufferings, which in our own career fell heavily upon us. It is difficult to dislodge this kind of selfishness from the heart. Indeed, there can hardly be a surer symptom of sound benevolence in a man, than his taking pleasure in those paths being smoothened which he will never have to traverse again: I do not say in making them smoother —it is much easier to reconcile himself to that—but in their being made so without his interference.

It would be well, indeed, if selfishness came into play on those occasions only where self is really concerned.

There is nothing which a wise employer will have more at heart than to gain the confidence of those under him. The essential requisites on his part are truth and kindness. These qualities may, however, belong in a high degree to persons who fail to gain the confidence of their dependents. In domestic life, confidence may be prevented by fits of capricious passion on the part of the ruling powers; and a man who, in all important matters, acts justly and kindly towards his family, may be deprived of their confidence by his weakness of temper in little things. For instance, you meet with persons who fall into a violent way of talking about all that offends them in their dependents; and who express themselves with as much anger about trivial inadvertencies as about serious moral offences. In the course of the same day that they have given way to some outbreak of temper, they may act with great self-denial and watchful kindness; but they can hardly expect their subordinates to be at ease with them. Another defect which prevents confidence, is a certain sterility of character, which does not allow of sympathy with other people's fancies and pursuits. A man of this character does not understand any likings but his own. He will be kind to you, if you will be happy in his way; but he has nothing but ridicule or coldness for any thing which does not suit him. This imperfection of sympathy, which prevents an equal from becoming a friend, may easily make a superior into a despot. Indeed, I almost doubt whether the head of a family does not do more mischief if he is unsympathetic, than even if he were unjust. The triumph of domestic rule is for the master's presence not to be felt as a restraint.

In a larger sphere than the domestic one, such as amongst the employers of labour and their men, the same elements are required on the part of the masters to produce confidence. Much frankness also and decisiveness are required. The more uneducated

people are, the more suspicious they are
likely to be: and the best way of meeting
this suspiciousness is to have as few conceal-
ments as possible; for instance, not to omit
stating any motives relating to your own interest as master, which may influence your
conduct towards your men.

There is a class of persons brought into
contact with the employers of labour and
their men, who might often do good service
to both, by endeavouring, when it is de-
served, to inspire the men with confidence
in the kindly intentions of their masters.
This is a duty which belongs to the clergy
and professional men in manufacturing towns.
There are many things which a man cannot
say for himself; and, as Bacon has observed,
it is one of the advantages of friendship, that
it provides some person to say these things
for one. So, in this case, it must often have
a very good effect, when a bystander, as it
were, explains to the men the kind wishes
and endeavours of a master manufacturer,
which explanation would come with much
less force and grace from the master himself.

I now come to a subject bordering on the
former, namely, the political confidence of
the operatives. I am afraid, that, at present,
there is a great distrust amongst them of
public men. This is not to be wondered at.
Their distrust is much fostered by the practice of imputing bad motives, and calling ill
names, so much the fashion in political writing of all kinds. It is not a vice peculiar
to this age : indeed, I question whether political writing has ever, upon the whole,
been more well-bred and considerate than
it is now. But at all times the abusive
style is the easiest mode of writing, and
the surest of sympathy. The skill to make,
and that to cure, a wound are different
things; but the former is the one which belongs to most people, and often attracts most
attention and encouragement. This, then,
is one cause of the distrust of the working
classes, which will only be mitigated by a
higher tone of moral feeling on the part of
the people generally. Another cause is to
be found in the unwise, if not dishonest, conduct of public men. Look at the mode of

proceeding at elections. I put aside bribery,
intimidation, and the like, the wrongfulness
of which I hope we are all agreed upon;
and I come to the intellectual part of the
business. Extreme opinions are put forth
by the candidates, often in violent and injurious language. Each strives to keep studiously in the background any points of difference between himself and the electing
body. Electors are not treated as rational
beings; their prejudices and their antipathies
are petted as if they belonged to some despot whom it was treason to contradict.
Whereas, if ever there is a time in his life
when a man should weigh his words well,
and when he should gird himself up to speak
with truth and courage, it is when he is soli-
citing the suffrages of an electoral body.
That is the way to anticipate inconsistency;
the crime of which is more often in the hasti-
ness of the first-formed opinion, than in the
change from it. What is called the inconsistency, may be the redeeming part of
the transaction. The candidate is naturally
tempted to fall in with the exact opinions
that are likely to ensure success, and to ex-

press them without modification—in fact, for
the sake of his present purpose, to leave as
little room for the exercise of his discretion
as possible. It is easy for him to make un-
conditional assertions, when nothing is to be
done upon them, but it is another thing when
he has to bring them into action. The direction which he may wish to give to public
affairs is likely to be met by many other impulses; and then he may have to remain
consistent and useless, or to link himself
to some friendly impulse which brings him,
however, into opposition to some of his
former broad and careless declarations. He
has left himself no room for using his judgment. Indeed, one does not see very clearly
why he takes his seat amongst men who are
met to deliberate. The evils that must arise
from rash promises at elections are so great,
that it is fortunate when the topics mooted
on those occasions, form but a small part of
those which ultimately come under the consideration of the person elected; and, as
often happens, that important public matters
come to be discussed, which were not seen on
the political horizon at the election time.

In addition to the distrust of individual legislators, which is, probably, frequent amongst the poorer classes, there is also, I suspect, a great distrust amongst them of the leading parties in the state. They perceive the evils of party, and see nothing on the other side. The meaning and intent of party, the way in which by its means social good is often worked out in a manner less harsh and abrupt, perhaps, than by any other means that has hitherto been devised, are considerations probably unknown to them. To address them upon such matters would be thought absurd. It would be said, that philosophical disquisitions on government are for the closet of the studious man, but not for common people coming to perform a plain, practical, duty. Great principles, however, are at the foundation of all good action. Look to the divine teaching. See how the highest things are addressed to all classes. There is no esoteric philosophy there—one thing to the initiated, and another to the outer populace. And so I am persuaded in addressing the great masses of mankind on other subjects, you can hardly be too profound, if you

contrive to express yourself without pe-
dantry; you can hardly put motives of too
much generosity before them, if you do so
with complete sincerity and earnestness. All
this is very difficult, but what social remedies are not? They are things to be toiled
and bled for; and what is far more, you
must run the risk of ridicule, endure want
of sympathy, have the courage to utter un-
palatable truths, and not unfrequently resist
the temptation of saying such things as are
sure to elicit immediate and hearty approba-
tion. When a statesman has a craving for
present applause, it is an evil spirit always
by his side, but which springs up to its utmost height, and overshadows him with its
most baneful influence, at some of the most
critical periods of his career.

But, in addition to the want of confidence
in public men caused by malicious writing,
or by their injudicious or dishonest conduct
as candidates, or by the ignorance amongst
the operatives of the good uses of party; is
there not also a just want of confidence
arising from the mode in which party warfare has sometimes been carried on in the

legislative body? Remember that it is possible to intrigue with " interests," as we call
them, as well as with private persons. The
nice morality which would shudder at the
revelations of petty intrigue disclosed by the
diary of a Bubb Doddington, may urge on,
and ride triumphantly, some popular cry, the
justice of which it has never paused to examine. There are also such things as a factious opposition to the Government, a selfish
desertion from it, or a slavish obedience to it;
which things, the people in general, are not
slow to note, and often prone to attribute,
even when there is no sufficient cause for at-
tributing them. But of all the things which
tend to separate the operatives from the governing classes, the most effectual, perhaps, is
the suspicion (oh, that we could say that it
was altogether an unjust one !) that laws are
framed, or maintained, which benefit those
classes at the expense of their poorer brethren.
We think it a marvellous act of malversation
in a trustee, to benefit himself unjustly out of
the funds entrusted to his care. Wrongs of
this kind may appear to be diluted when the
national prosperity is the trust-fund, and the

legislative body is the trustee. The largeness, however, of the transaction, does not
diminish the injustice of it, although it may
soothe the conscience, or partially excuse the
conduct of any individual member of the
governing class. By governing class, I do
not merely mean the legislative bodies, but I
include the electing body, who are of course
equally guilty when they clamour for what
they deem their own peculiar interest, instead
of calling for just laws. And they may be
sure, that when once the great mass of the
people are persuaded that the injustice which
I have spoken of, is a ruling principle in any
government; that government, if it lives, is
henceforth based upon fear, and not upon
affection.

I SHALL now put down a few points of practice, which, though they are classed together, have no other link than that they all relate to our conduct in a family and towards dependents.

In social government, no less than in legislating for a state, there should be constant reference to great principles, if only from the exceeding difficulty of foreseeing, or appreciating, the results in detail of any measure.

It is a foolish thing when a man so guides himself, that it is generally supposed in his family, and among his dependents, that no arguments of theirs are likely to persuade him to alter his views. Such a one may fancy that what he calls his firmness is the main stay of his authority: but the obstinacy, which never listens, is not less fatal than the facility which never listens but to yield. If your rule has the reputation of not being amenable to reason, it is liable to sudden convulsions and headstrong distempers, or to unreasonable cringings, in which your welfare, and that of those whom you rule, are sacrificed to the apprehension of provoking your self-will. Moreover, the fear of irrational opposition on your part, often tempts those about you into taking up courses, which, otherwise, they might have thrown aside upon reflection, or after reasonable converse with you on the subject. You may have, in the end, to oppose yourself sternly to the wishes of those whom you would guide wisely; but at any rate give yourself the chance of having, in the first instance, the full effect of any forces in their own minds which may be on your side. You cannot expect to have these useful allies, if your wont is to be blindly obstinate, and to carry things, on all occasions, by heavy-handed authority. The way in which expected opposition acts in determining the mind, is not always by creating immediate wilfulness: but a man, knowing that there is sure to be objection made, in any particular quarter, to his taking a course, respecting which he has not made up his own mind, sets to work to put aside that

contingent obstacle to his freedom of action.
In doing this, however, he generates, as it
were, a force in the opposite direction : in
arguing against contingent opposition, he is
led to make assertions which he is ashamed
to draw back from; and so, in the end, he
fails to exercise an unbiassed judgment.   I
have gone minutely into this matter; but it
cannot be unimportant for those who rule,
to consider well the latent sources of human
motive.

In addressing persons of inferior station,
do not be prone to suppose that there is
much occasion for intellectual condescension
on your part : at any rate do not be careless
in what you say, as if any thing would do
for them.   Observe the almost infinite fleet-
ness of your own powers of thought, and
then consider whether it is likely that education has much to do with this.   Use simple
language, but do not fear to put substance
in it : choose, if you like, common materials,
but make the best structure that you can
of them : and be assured that method and

logical order are not thrown away upon any one. The rudest audience, as well as the most refined, soon grows weary, I suspect, of protracted, driftless, tautology.

Do not dwell more than you can help, upon the differences of nature between yourself and those with whom you live. Consider whether your own vanity is not too requiring. See that others have not the same complaint to make of your uncongeniality, that you are, perhaps, prone to make of theirs. If you are, indeed, superior, reckon it as your constant duty, to try and sympathize with those beneath you; to mix with their pursuits, as far as you can, and thus, insensibly, to elevate them. Perhaps there is no mind that will not yield some return for your labour: it seems the dullest, bleakest, rock, not earth enough to feed a nettle; yet up grows, with culture, the majestic pine.

A want of sympathy leads to the greatest ignorance in the intellect as well as in the heart.

Remember that your dependents have sel-

dom a full power of replying to you ; and let
the recollection of that make you especially
considerate in your dealings with them.

When you find a lack of truth in those
about you, consider whether it may not arise
from the furiousness of your own temper
which scares truth away from you : and reflect how fearful a part the angry man may
have in the sin of those falsehoods which
immoderate fear of him gives rise to.   Such,
I am afraid, is the tyrannous nature of the
human heart that we not only show, but really
feel, more anger at offence given us by those
under our power, than at any other cause
whatever.

It is a mistake to suppose that we necessarily become indifferent to the faults and
foibles of those with whom we live : on the
contrary, we sometimes grow more and more
alive to them : they seem, as it were, to create
a corresponding soreness in ourselves : and,
knowing that they exist in the character, we
are apt to fancy that we perceive them even

on occasions when they are not in the least brought into play.

Do not be fond of the display of authority, or think that there is anything grand in being obeyed with abject fear. One certainly meets with persons who are vain of their ill-temper, and of seeing how it keeps the people about them in order; a species of vanity which they might share with any wild animal at large.

In reasoning with your dependants, do not allow yourself to make broad assertions and careless conclusions, merely because you are addressing inferiors. " The Courts of Reason recognise no difference of persons." And when you wish to disabuse the minds of those entrusted to your guidance of any thing which you are convinced is erroneous, do not attempt to do so by unmeasured condemnation. It is seldom that a secure answer is given to any theory, or system, except by one who exhausts, and lays before you, the good in it.

Let not your forgiveness be of that kind which may almost be set down as forgetfulness.

You must not always expect to hear a good explanation of a man's reason for his conduct. In the first place, he does not carry such things about with him in a producible shape; some of them he has probably forgotten, although their influence may still remain strongly upon his mind; and such as he does give, are likely to be those which he thinks will have most weight with the person to whom he is speaking.

In giving way to selfish persons, remember that you cannot sacrifice yourself alone. Any relation in which you may be placed to them, especially if you are the superior, is not a thing that concerns you only; but is, as it were, a trust for society in general.

It is hard to judge about quarrels, for the points on which they openly break out have often no more to do with the real grounds of difference than the place of a battle with the cause of the war. Many a quarrel, after running for a long time under ground, gushes forth with a vehemence which seems unaccountable; and it is difficult to divine what lands it has passed through in its hidden course. Any particular outbreak cannot safely be taken as an index of the general conduct of the parties towards each other.

Playfulness is a good means of softening social distances. A stiff, grave, man is always in danger of being feared too much. On the other hand, as the self-love of many people is suspicious in the extreme, you must expect that your most innocent playfulness will often be mistaken for ridicule.

It is a duty not to allow yourself to think of any living man, still less to treat him, as if your hopes of his amendment were utterly dead and gone.

You must not be much surprised at the ingratitude of those to whom you have given nothing but money.

Once give your mind to suspicion, and there will be sure to be food enough for it. In the stillest night, the air is filled with sounds for the wakeful ear that is resolved to listen.

A misproud man resolves to abide by the evil words which he has spoken in anger. This freezing of foam is wilfully unnatural; and turns a brief madness into a settled insanity.

A man of any wisdom, in domestic authority, so far from making large claims to the love of those whom he rules, and exacting all manner of observance as his due, will often think with fear how unworthy he is of the affection even of the dullest and least-gifted creature about him.

In commenting on any error of an agent or dependant, beware of making your own vexation, and not the real offence, the measure of your blame. This is a most frequent source of injustice, and one, moreover, which tends to prevent anything like consistent training.

The poor, the humble, and your dependants, will often be afraid to ask their due from you : be the more mindful of it yourself.

With what degree of satisfaction do you feel that you could meet those persons in a future state over whom you have any influence now? Your heart's answer to this question is somewhat of a test of your behaviour towards them.

How ready we should often be to forgive those who are angry with us, if we could only see how much of their anger arises from vexation with themselves for having begun to be angry at all.

I am not sorry to introduce a maxim, like the above, which relates, perhaps, rather more to dependants than to those in authority, and which claims a place among precepts on social government, only as it may tend to promote social harmony and peace. I have not attempted, throughout, to give any account of the duties of dependants,

which, however, are easily inferred as sup-
plementary to the duties of masters. It is
not to be supposed that any relation in life
is one-sided, that kindness is to be met by
indifference, or that loyalty to those who lead
us is not a duty of the highest order. But,
fortunately, the proneness of men to regard
with favour those put in authority over them is
very strong; and I have but little fear of finding
any large body of thoughtful and kind masters suffering from permanent indifference, or
ingratitude, on the part of their dependants.

I cannot close the chapter better than by
entreating those, who are endeavouring to
carry on any system of benevolence, to be
very watchful in the management of details,
and to strengthen themselves against any
feelings of disgust and weariness which may
encroach upon them, when their undertaking
has lost the attraction of novelty. Details
are like the fibres at the root of a tree : without their aid the tree would have but little
hold against the wind : they are the channels
for its terrestrial nutriment ; they are its ties
to earth, its home and birth-place ; and, in-

significant as they seem, it could live almost
better without light than without them. Here
it is that practical wisdom comes in—that
faculty, without which, the greatest gifts may
serve to make a noise and a flame, and nothing more. It holds its object neither too
near, nor too far off; without exaggerating
trifles, it can see that small things may be
essential to the successful application of great
principles; it is moderate in its expectations;
does not imagine that all men must be full of
its projects; and holds its course with calm-
ness, with hope, and with humility.

You must not enter upon a career of usefulness without expecting innumerable vexations and crosses to affect the details of any
project or system you may undertake. And
when the novelty of your purpose has somewhat worn off, and you have to meet with the
honest opposition of other minds, as well as
to contend against their vanity, their selfishness, and their unreasonableness, it requires
a high and full source for your benevolence
to flow from, if it would bear down these
annoyances. Even when they cannot dry up
the stream, or change its current, if you are

not watchful over yourself, they may make it flow more feebly. The very prospect of success is to some minds a great temptation to make them slacken their efforts. Throughout the course of our pursuit, we are never, perhaps, so prone to be weary and to repine, as when we begin to feel sure of ultimate success, but at the same time to perceive, that a long and definite period must elapse before the completion of our undertaking.

Against the many temptations that beset a man in such a career, I do not believe that any good feeling, which stands upon no other than mere human relations, will be found a sufficient support. No sentimental benevolence will do; nor even, at all times, a warm and earnest philanthropy: there must be the inexorable sense of duty arising from a man's apprehension, if but in a feeble degree, of his relation towards God, as well as to his fellow man.

CHAPTER III.

Labour in Factories.

THE two former chapters have been given to the consideration of the relation between the employer of labour and the labouring man, and to general reflections upon the duties arising from that relation. Let us now take a particular instance, the employment of labour in manufactures for example, and go through some of the more obvious points to which the master might in that case direct his attention beneficially.

1. The Mill.

IT would seem an obvious thing enough, that when a man collects a number of his fellow-men together to work for him, it would be right to provide a sufficient supply of air for them.

But this does not appear to have been considered as an axiom; and, in truth, we cannot much wonder at this neglect, when we find that those who have to provide for the amusement of men, and who would be likely, therefore to consult the health and convenience of those whom they bring together, should sedulously shut out the pure air, as if they disliked letting anything in that did not pay for admission. In most grievances, the people aggrieved are very sensible at the time of the evil they are undergoing; which is not, however, the case with those who suffer from an impure atmosphere. They are, in general, almost unconscious of what they are enduring. This makes it the more desirable, in the case we are considering, that the manufacturer himself, or the government, or the community at large, should be alive to the mischief arising from want of ventilation in these crowded assemblages of men, and to the absolute necessity of providing remedies for it.

This will not be an inappropriate place for saying something about the non-interference principle. There is no doubt that interfe-

rence has often been most tyrannous and
absurd, that our ancestors, for instance,
sometimes interfered only to insist upon im-
possibilities, and that we may occasionally
do the same.   But, on the other hand, the
let-alone principle proceeds upon the sup-
position, not only that every body knows his
own interest best, or if not, that his freedom
of action is of more importance than his acting wisely, which is often true ; but it also
goes on to assume that every body knows
and will take just care of the welfare of
others.   Push either principle to any great
length ; and you will find yourself in the
land of confusion and absurdity.   In truth,
I should seldom like to say anything about
the wisdom, or the folly, of interference, until
I knew exactly what it was about, and how far
you intended to interfere.   It is one of those
matters in which it is especially desirable to
keep in mind those maxims of prudence,
respecting the application of general rules to
moral questions, which Burke has handled
so admirably.   " Nothing universal," he ob-
serves, " can be rationally affirmed on any
" moral, or any political subject.   Pure me-

" taphysical abstraction does not belong to
" these matters. The lines of morality are
" not like ideal lines of mathematicks. They
" are broad and deep as well as long. They
" admit of exceptions; they demand modifica-
" tions. These exceptions and modifications
" are not made by the process of logic, but
" by the rules of prudence. Prudence is
" not only the first in rank of the virtues
" political and moral, but she is the director,
" the regulator, the standard of them all."
To take a particular instance of legislative
interference, namely, the enactments about
building party-walls, can any one doubt that
this interference has been most beneficial?
Does any one suppose that, without it, the
same good results would have been gained?
Would the prudence of private individuals ever
have accomplished it? Besides, I think it can
hardly be denied that a state should have a
degree of providence for the general body,
not to be expected from private individuals,
and which might compel them to do things
that would not consort with their interest
even upon the most enlarged views which
they could take of it. The financial affairs

of the nation are conducted with no slight
apparatus of intrusion and vexation. We
endure this patiently: indeed, in many cases,
it is difficult to see how it could be obviated.
Surely we may submit to some simple sanitary regulations, especially of that kind which
may be compared to indirect taxation, requiring to be attended to only by a certain
class of persons of daily experience in the
matter. Such are regulations with respect
to building, which need to be looked to in the
first instance; and then the results of them
remain for ever afterwards a great gain to
public health and morals. I am speaking
now rather of the question of annoyance, than
of loss, from legislative interference. Of
course, in this matter of building, it is easy
to perceive that limits must carefully be put
to the extent of interference with a view to
keeping down the expense. If this is not done,
the whole purpose of the regulations may be
defeated. But even in this, it is possible to
be too nice with respect to interfering with
what are called the rights of property, or too
much afraid of creating an artificial dearness

by regulations, many of which will in the end be found to be a great saving.

But to resume the subject of the Mill. Each branch of manufactures has its peculiar dangers and disadvantages; and it behoves the master to be frequently directing his attention to remedy the peculiar evils of his manufacture. He is to be the pioneer to find out for his men ways of avoiding these evils. It cannot be his duty to study only how to make his fabric cheaper, and not to take any pains to see how it can be made to cost less of human life. However, if a man has once got a just view of his position as an employer of labour, he will not need to be urged in this matter, but must see at once that the health of his men is one of the first things for him to look to. What would you think of a commander who was careless of the health of his army, merely because he had an indefinite power of recruiting? In a thickly-peopled country like this, an employer of labour, if his work does not require much skill, can generally get any number of men to serve him, which would be a strange reason, however, for making the health of any one amongst those whom he does employ less precious in his eyes. Human labour may be ever so abundant, but human life cannot be cheap.

While we are talking of the Mill, it may be well to observe that the system of piece-work, when it is done by a man with children under him, is likely to be made too severe work for them. It is a hard fate, indeed, for children to be always under the eye of one whose interest it is to get as much work out of them as possible. The above remarks, however, apply even more to piece-work done at home than at the mill.

The next thing to be mentioned in con-nexion with the Mill is the time of labour. This is a great question, embracing many considerations which it would be quite foreign to my purpose to enter upon here. But I may observe that there is much in this matter which might be done by the masters, indi-vidually, and collectively. They have to con-sider how the time that they may get for the recreation of their men is to be apportioned. For instance, whether it is better to give it

in whole days, or by half-days, or to spread
it over the ordinary days of work. These
are questions that cannot be answered without much thought and knowledge respecting
the social habits of the labouring people.

All that we have addressed to the manufacturer on the subject of his Mill, applies
even more cogently to the minor superintendent of labour and his workshop. There,
the evils complained of are often far greater.
Ventilation is less attended to; less pains
are taken to diminish the peculiar dangers of
the craft; the hours of labour are more numerous; and the children sometimes exposed
to cruelties utterly unheard of in factories.
Read the evidence respecting the employment of milliners, and you will wish that
dresses could be made up, as well as the
materials made for them, in factories. Alas!
what a striking instance the treatment of
these poor milliner girls is of the neglect
of duty on the part of employers: I mean
of those who immediately superintend this
branch of labour, and of those who cause
it. Had the former been the least aware of
their responsibility, would they have hesi-

tated to remonstrate against the unreasonable orders of their customers? And, as for
the latter, for the ladies who expect such
orders to be complied with, how sublimely
inconsiderate of the comfort of those beneath
them they must have become. I repeat it
again: the careless cruelty in the world almost
outweighs the rest.

2. The School-room.

Some manufacturer may think that this branch
of the matter does not belong to him, as he does
not employ children of the age which makes
it incumbent upon him by law to have anything to do with their schooling. But I would
venture to suggest that it is a matter which
belongs to all of us, and, especially, to those
who are able to pay attention to the habits of
large masses of people, put, as it were, under
their care. Suppose that there had been no
such thing in the world's history as a decline
and fall of the Roman Empire. In the course
of time, though we should probably have had
our Domitians and our Neros, we might
have delighted in a modern Trajan or an

Antonine. Under such a man, the progress
of letters having proceeded in any thing like
the manner that it has done, we should have
had some general system of national education, which, after the Roman fashion of com-
pleteness, would have traversed the state,
with iron step, doubtless even to the remote
ends of barbarian Britain. To say that this
would not have been a signal benefit to mankind would be idle: what we have to say
against the despotic system is, that it absorbs
private virtue, and suppresses private endeavour; that, though it may create better
machines, it certainly makes worse men.
Now then to bring these imaginings home;
for they do concern us closely. My readers
are, to a certain extent, educated; they will
have gained by living in a free state; but
if they continue to neglect the welfare of
the great mass, in respect of education,
can they say that this, the first layer of
the nation, the " turba Remi," might not
almost wish, if they could comprehend the
question, to live under a despot who would
educate them, rather than with free men
who do not? Are we to enjoy the singular

freedom of speech and action, which we do enjoy in this country, and to expect to have no sacrifice to make for it? Is liberty, the first of possessions, to have no duties corresponding to its invaluable rights? And, in fine, ought it not to be some drawback on the enjoyment of our own freedom, if a doubt can come across our minds whether a vast mass of our fellow citizens might not be the better for living under a despotic government? These are very serious questions; and the sooner we are able, with a good conscience, to give a satisfactory answer to them, the better. Till that time, let no man in this country say that the education of the people is nothing to him.

But how strange it is that men should require to be urged to this good work of education. The causing children to be taught is a thing so full of joy, of love, of hope, that one wonders how such a gladsome path of benevolence could ever have been unfrequented. The delight of educating is like that of cultivating near the fruitful Nile, where seed time and harvest come so close together. And when one looks forward to the indefinite extension that any efforts in this direction may probably enjoy, one is apt to feel as if nothing else were important, and to be inclined to expend all one's energies in this one course. Indeed, it is hard to estimate the enormous benefit of enabling a man to commune with the most exalted minds of all time, to read the most significant records of all ages, to find that others have felt and seen and suffered as himself, to extend his sympathy with his brother-man, his insight into nature, his knowledge of the ways of God. Now the above is but a poor description of what the humblest education offers.

Let us now consider the subject of " the school-room" more in detail. And, the first remark I have to make, is, that we should perpetually recal to mind the nature of our own thoughts, and sensations, at the early periods of life in which those are whom we are trying to educate. This will make us careful not to weary children with those things which we long to impress most upon them. The repetition of words, whatever they may contain, is often like the succession of waves in a receding tide, which makes less

of an inroad at each pulsation. It is different
when an idea, or state of feeling, is repeated
by conduct of various kinds: that is most
impressive. If a child, for instance, is brought
up where there is a pervading idea of any
kind, manifested as it will be in many ways,
the idea is introduced again and again without wearisomeness, and the child imbibes
it unconsciously. But mere maxims, embracing this idea, would very likely have
gained no additional influence with him from
being constantly repeated: that is, at the
time; for, in after years, the maxims may,
perhaps, fasten upon his mind with a peculiar strength, simply from their having been
often repeated to him at an early period of
his life. But at present this repetition may
be of immense disservice. You cannot continue to produce the same effect by words,
that you did on first using them; and often
you go on hammering about a thing until
you loosen what was fast in the first instance.
It is well to keep such reflections steadily in
mind as regards religious instruction for the
young, and, especially, as regards religious
services for them. Go back to your own

youth, and recollect how little command of
attention you had yourself, how volatile you
were, how anxious to escape all tedium, how
weary of words, how apt to dislike routine.
Then see whether you make sufficient allowance for these feelings in dealing with the
young; and whether it might not be possible
to give them the same holy precepts, to com-
municate the same extent, or nearly so, of
religious instruction, and yet to ensure their
love for the times, and places, and circumstances, of this communication. You must
allow that you do a very dangerous thing
indeed, when you make that wearisome which
you wish to be most loved. I must confess
that it has often struck me, that we insist
upon too much religious attendance from
children of a tender age; and, considering
what we know of the impatience of the human mind, I cannot but think that such a
system is often most prejudicial. I say these
things with much hesitation, and some fear
of being misunderstood; and I do not venture to enter into details, or to presume to
say what should be the exact course in so
difficult a question. What I wish, is to

draw the attention of those engaged in instruction to a point of view which may sometimes escape them, or which they may be
tempted to neglect for the sake of appearances, the household gods of this generation.

There is one maxim which those who superintend schools should ponder well; and that
is, that the best things to be learnt are those
which the children cannot be examined upon.
One cannot but fear that the masters will be
apt to think school-proficiency all in all; and
that the founders and supporters of schools
will, occasionally, be tempted by vanity to
take most interest in those things which give
most opportunity for display. Yet the slightest
inferiority of moral tone in a school would
be ill compensated for by an expertness, almost marvellous, in dealing with figures; or a
knowledge of names, things, and places, which
may well confound the grown-up bystander.
That school would in reality be the one to
be proud of, where order was thoroughly
maintained with the least admixture of fear;
where you would have most chance of meet-

ing with truthful replies from the children in
a matter where such replies would criminate
themselves : and where you would find the
most kindly feeling to each other prevalent
throughout. Yet these are things not to be
seen on show days, that cannot be got up
for exhibition, that require unwearied supervision on the part of masters and benefactors,
that will never be attempted but by those
who, themselves, feel deeply the superiority
of moral excellence to all else. Such teachers
will see how the kindness of children to each
other may be encouraged. They will take
more notice of a good-natured thing than
a clever one. They will show, how much,
even in the minutest trifles, truth and forti-
tude weigh with them. They will be careful
not to stimulate an unwholesome craving for
praise in their pupils. They will look not
only to the thing done, but also to the mode
and spirit of doing it. That this spirit and
mode may be the means of generating and
guiding future endeavour will be a main
object with such instructors. The dignity of
labour, the independence of thrift, the greatness of contentment, will be themes dwelt

upon by them, in their loving foresight for the future welfare of the infant labourers entrusted to their care. To endear holy things to these little ones would delight such teachers far more than to instil the utmost proficiency in any critical or historical knowledge of the sacred writings. Not that the two things are in the least degree incompatible. Far from it, indeed! All I mean to insist on is, that such teachers will perceive what are the great objects of culture: and how subservient even the best knowledge is to the apprehension of duty. They will see, too, more clearly the necessity of bearing in mind the pre-eminence of moral and religious culture, when they reflect that many of their pupils come from places which cannot be called homes, where scarcely anything like parental love sustains or informs them, and where, perhaps, confusion, discontent, and domestic turbulence prevail.

We may remark, as bearing upon this subject, that singing lessons should be greatly encouraged in schools. There are several merits connected with this mode of instruction. It employs many together, and gives a

feeling of communion; it is not much mixed
up with emulation; the tenderest and highest
sentiments may be unostentatiously impressed
by its means, for you can introduce in songs
such things as you could not lecture upon;
then it gives somewhat of a cultivated taste,
and an additional topic of social interest, even
to those who do not make much proficiency;
while to others, who have a natural ability
for it, it may form an innocent and engaging
pursuit throughout their lives.

With respect to the intellectual part of
teaching, I have not much to say : and it is
a branch of the subject which has engaged,
and is engaging, the attention of men who
are much more capable of speaking about it
than I am. The only thing which it occurs
to me to mention is, that one would like to
see a great deal of manual teaching, with a
view not only to the future profit, but also
to the future pleasure and instruction of the
children. When you think that many of them
will be artisans, whose only occupation, perhaps, will be to perform some one process of
manufactures, requiring next to no thought
or skill, it becomes the more necessary to

educate their hands as well as their heads.
Man is an animal very fond of construction
of any sort; and a wise teacher, knowing
the happiness that flows from handiwork, will
seize upon opportunities for teaching even
the most trivial accomplishments of a manual
kind. They will come in, hereafter, to embellish a man's home, and to endear it to
him. They will occupy time that would,
otherwise, be ill spent. And, besides, there
are many persons whose cleverness lies only
in this way; and you have to teach them this
or nothing.

3. The Playground.

This is a place quite as important as the
school-room. Here it is, that a large part of
the moral cultivation may be carried on. It
is a great object to humanize the conduct of
children to each other at play times without
interfering with them, or controlling them,
too much. But we have, before, gone over
the motives which should actuate a teacher
in his moral guidance; and it needs only to
remark, that the playground is a place where

that guidance is eminently required; and
where the exigencies for it are most easily
discerned.

Those games should not be overlooked
which are of a manly kind, and likely to be
continued in after life. This brings us naturally to think of the playgrounds for children of a larger growth. Hitherto there has
been a sad deficiency in this matter in our
manufacturing towns, and almost everywhere
else. Can any thing be more lamentable to
contemplate than a dull, grim, and vicious
population, whose only amusement is sen-
suality? Yet, what can we expect, if we
provide no means whatever of recreation; if
we never share our own pleasures with our
poorer brethren; and if the public buildings
which invite them in their brief hours of leisure
are chiefly gin palaces? As for our cathedrals and great churches, we mostly have
them well locked up, for fear any one should
steal in and say a prayer, or contemplate
a noble work of art, without paying for
it: and we shut people up by thousands in
dense towns with no outlets to the country,
but those which are guarded on each side

by dusty hedges. Now an open space near a town is one of nature's churches: and it is an imperative duty to provide such things. Nor, indeed, should we stop at giving breathing places to crowded multitudes in great towns. To provide cheap locomotion, as a means of social improvement, should be ever in the minds of legislators and other influential persons. Blunders in legislating about railroads, and absurd expenditure in making them, are a far greater public detriment than they may seem at first sight. Again, without interfering too much, or attempting to force a "Book of Sports" upon the people, who in that case, would be resolutely dull and lugubrious, the benevolent employer of labour might exert himself in many ways to encourage healthful and instructive amusements amongst his men. He might give prizes for athletic excellence or skill. He might aid in establishing zoological gardens, or music-meetings, or exhibitions of pictures, or mechanics' institutes. These are things in which some of the great employers of labour have already set him the example. Let him remember how much his workpeople are deprived of by being almost confined to one spot; and let him be the more anxious to enlarge their minds by inducing them to take interest in any thing which may prevent the " ignorant present," and its low cares, from absorbing all their attention. He has very likely some pursuit, or some art, in which he takes especial pleasure himself, and which gives to his leisure, perhaps, its greatest charm: he may be sure that there are many of his people who could be made to share in some degree that pleasure, or pursuit, with him. It is a large, a sure, and certainly a most pleasurable beneficence, to provide for the poor such opportunities of recreation, or means of amusement, as I have mentioned above. Neither can it be set down as at all a trifling matter. Depend upon it, that man has not made any great progress in humanity who does not care for the leisure hours and amusements of his fellow-men.

While we are upon this matter, I will mention something which borders closely upon it, though it applies to the consumer rather than the manufacturer. Most men would think it much, if it were brought home to them, that from any carelessness of theirs, some person had suffered unnecessary imprisonment, if only for a day.   And yet any one, who encourages unreasonably late hours of business, does what he can to uphold a system of needless confinement, depriving thousands of that healthful change of pursuit which is one of the main aliments both for body and soul, and leaving little time or opportunity for any thing to grow up in their minds beyond the rudest and most trivial cares and objects.

4. The Workman's Home.

That the workman should have a home, which, however humble it may be, should yet afford room and scope for the decencies, if not for some of the comforts and refinements of civilized life, is manifestly essential, if we wish to preserve the great body of the people from a state of savageness. There is an important and original remark on this subject in the Hand Loom Weavers Report of 1841 :

" The man who dines for 6d. and clothes himself during
" the year for £5. is probably as healthily fed, and as

" healthily clad, as if his dinner cost two guineas a day,
" and his dress £200 a year.   But this is not the case
" with respect to habitation.   Every increase of accom-
" modation, from the corner of a cellar to a mansion,
" renders the dwelling more healthy, and, to a consider-
" able extent, the size and goodness of the dwelling
" tends to render its inmates more civilized."

Indeed, if civilization does not show itself in
a man's home, where else is it likely to take
much root with him?   Make his home comfortable, and you do more towards making
him a steady and careful citizen, than you
could by any other means.   Now only look
around, and see how entirely this has been
neglected, at least, until within a recent date.
Our workers are toiling all day long, or, if
they have leisure, it is mostly accompanied
by pecuniary distress: and can you expect
in either case that they will busy themselves
about those primary structural arrangements
without which it is scarcely possible to have
a comfortable home?   Many of the things,
too, which are needful for this end, require
capital, or, at least, such conjoint enterprise
as can hardly be expected from the poor.
Take any individual workman.   Suppose
there is defective drainage in his street, or,

as often happens, no drainage at all, what can one such man do, even if at all alive to the evil? When you consider the dependent condition of the labouring classes, and how little time they have for domestic arrangements of any kind, does it not behove the employer of labour to endeavour that his workmen should have opportunities of getting places to live in, fit for human beings in a civilized country? I use the phrase " employer of labour," in its widest sense; and at once say, that there are many things bearing upon the comfort of the habitations of the poor, which both the local authorities and the imperial government ought to look to. Is there not a strange mockery in the fact, stated in the Sanitary Report, that " the " annual slaughter in England and Wales " from preventible causes of typhus which " attacks persons in the vigour of life, ap- " pears to be double the amount of what was " suffered by the allied armies in the battle " of Waterloo?" Must we not say again that the careless cruelty of the world almost outweighs the rest?

I have hitherto abstained from vexing my

readers with details; nor do I wish now to
do more than draw their attention to a few
extracts from public documents respecting the
habitations of the poor. I take the following from the Hand Loom Weavers' Report
in 1841.

" The First Annual Report of the Registrar-General,
showed for the year 1838 a variation of the annual mortality in different districts of the metropolis, amounting
to 100 per cent.; a difference nearly equal to that which
exists between the most healthy and the least healthy
portions of the world. The inquiries instituted at the
same time by the Poor Law Commissioners into the
physical causes of fever in the metropolis, have traced
the comparative mortality of the unhealthy districts principally to the presence of impurities, the want of ventilation, and the bad construction of houses.

" The following extracts from Dr. Southwood Smith's
Report on Bethnal Green and Whitechapel, show both
the causes and the intensity of the evil.

' It appears,' says Dr. Southwood Smith, 'that in many
' parts of Bethnal Green and Whitechapel, fever of a ma-
' lignant and fatal character is always more or less pre-
' valent. In some streets it has recently prevailed in
' almost every house; in some courts in every house;
' and in some few instances in every room in every
' house. Cases are recorded in which every member
' of a family has been attacked in succession, of whom
' in every such case several have died; some whole
' families have been swept away. Instances are de-

' tailed in which there have been found in one small
' room six persons lying ill of fever together; I have
' myself seen this, four in one bed, and two in another.

* * * * * * * *

' The room of a fever patient in a small and heated apart-
' ment in London, with no perflation of fresh air, is per-
' fectly analogous to a standing pool in Ethiopia full of
' bodies of dead locusts. The poison generated in both
' cases is the same; the difference is merely in the degree
' of its potency. Nature with her burning sun, her stilled
' and pent up wind, her stagnant and teeming marsh,
' manufactures plague on a large and fearful scale. Po-
' verty in her hut, covered with her rags, surrounded
' with her filth, striving with all her might to keep out
' the pure air and to increase the heat, imitates nature
' but too successfully: the process and the product are
' the same; the only difference is in the magnitude of
' the result.

' But the magnitude of the result in London, if that
' magnitude be estimated by the numbers attacked, is
' not slight. From returns received from the Bethnal
' Green and Whitechapel Unions it appears that during
' the last year there occurred of fever cases,

' In the Bethnal Green Union . . 2,084
' In the Whitechapel Union . . . 2,557
_____

' Total . . 4,641'

The state of things described above by Dr.
Southwood Smith is by no means confined to
the metropolis; nor, even, is it to be seen in
its worst form there. Mr. Chadwick says,

" the most wretched of the stationary popu-
" lation of which I have been able to obtain
" any account, or that I have ever seen, was
" that which I saw in company with Dr.
" Arnott, and others, in the wynds of Edin-
" burgh and Glasgow." I forbear to add
their detailed report, which, as regards Glasgow especially, represents a loathsome state
of filth and wretchedness. If we go now to
the manufacturing towns of England, the evidence is of a similar character. " The fol-
" lowing extract," says the Sanitary Report,
" is descriptive of the condition of large
" classes of tenements in the manufacturing
" towns of Lancashire. It is from the report
" of Mr. Pearson, the medical officer of the
" Wigan Union."

" From the few observations which I have been en-
" abled to make respecting the causes of fever during the
" two months which I have held the situation of house-
" surgeon to the Dispensary, I am inclined to consider
" the filthy condition of the town as being the most pro-
" minent source. Many of the streets are unpaved and
" almost covered with stagnant water, which lodges in
" numerous large holes which exist upon their surface,
" and into which the inhabitants throw all kinds of re-
" jected animal and vegetable matters, which then un-
" dergo decay and emit the most poisonous exhalations.

" These matters are often allowed, from the filthy habits
" of the inhabitants of these districts, many of whom,
" especially the poor Irish, are utterly regardless both of
" personal and domestic cleanliness, to accumulate to
" an immense extent, and thus become prolific sources
" of malaria, rendering the atmosphere an active poison."

Dr. Edward Knight, speaking of some parts
of the town of Stafford, says,

" These parts of the town are without drainage, the
" houses, which are private property, are built without
" any regard to situation or ventilation, and constructed
" in a manner to ensure the greatest return at the least
" possible outlay. The accommodation in them does
" not extend beyond two rooms; these are small, and,
" for the most part, the families work in the day-time in
" the same room in which they sleep, to save fuel.

" There is not any provision made for refuse dirt,
" which, as the least trouble, is thrown down in front of
" the houses, and there left to putrefy."

Mr. William Rayner, the medical officer of
the Heaton Norris district of the Stockport
Union, thus describes a part of that town :

" There are forty-four houses in the two rows, and
" twenty-two cellars, all of the same size. The cellars
" are let off as separate dwellings; these are dark, damp,
" and very low, not more that six feet between the ceil-
" ing and floor. The street between the two rows is
" seven yards wide, in the centre of which is the common
" gutter, or more properly sink, into which all sorts of

" refuse is thrown ; it is a foot in depth. Thus there is
" always a quantity of putrefying matter contaminating
" the air. At the end of the rows is a pool of water very
" shallow and stagnant, and a few yards further, a part
" of the town's gas works. In many of these dwellings
" there are four persons in one bed."

We might have hoped that country districts
at least would have been free from the evils
occasioned by contracted building, want of
ventilation, want of drainage, and the like ;
but this is far indeed from being the case.
The following is from the report of Mr.
Aaron Little, the medical officer of the Chip-
penham Union :

" The parish of Colerne, which, upon a cursory view,
" any person (unacquainted with its peculiarities) would
" pronounce to be the most healthy village in England,
" is in fact the most unhealthy. From its commanding
" position (being situated upon a high hill) it has an ap-
" pearance of health and cheerfulness which delights the
" eye of the traveller, who commands a view of it from
" the Great Western road ; but this impression is imme-
" diately removed on entering at any point of the town.
" The filth, the dilapidated buildings, the squalid ap-
" pearance of the majority of the lower orders, have a
" sickening effect upon the stranger who first visits this
" place. During three years' attendance on the poor of
" this district, I have never known the small pox, scar-
" latina, or the typhus fever to be absent. The situation

" is damp, and the buildings unhealthy, and the inha-
" bitants themselves inclined to be of dirty habits. There
" is also a great want of drainage."

Mr. John Fox, the medical officer of the
Cerne Union, Dorsetshire, gives the following evidence :

" In many of the cottages, where synochus prevailed,
" the beds stood on the ground-floor, which was damp
" three parts of the year; scarcely one had a fire place in
" the bed-room, and one had a single small pane of
" glass stuck in the mud wall as its only window, with
" a large heap of wet and dirty potatoes in one corner.
" Persons living in such cottages are generally very
" poor, very dirty, and usually in rags; living almost
" wholly on bread and potatoes, scarcely ever tasting
" animal food, and consequently highly susceptible of
" disease and very unable to contend with it. I am
" quite sure if such persons were placed in good, com-
" fortable, clean cottages, the improvement in themselves
" and children would soon be visible, and the exceptions
" would only be found in a few of the poorest and most
" wretched, who perhaps had been born in a mud hovel,
" and had lived in one the first thirty years of their
" lives."

Mr. James Gane, the medical officer of the
Uxbridge Union, says,

" I attribute the prevalence of diseases of an epidemic
" character, which exists so much more among the poor
" than among the rich, to be, from the want of better

" accommodation as residence, (their dwellings instead
" of being built of solid materials are complete shells of
" mud on a spot of waste land the most swampy in the
" parish ; this is to be met with almost everywhere in
" rural districts) to the want of better clothing, being
" better fed, more attention paid to the cleanliness of
" their dwellings, and less congregated together."

Mr. Thomas H. Smith, the medical officer
of the Bromley Union, states :

" My attention was first directed to the sources of
" malaria in this district and neighbourhood when cho-
" lera became epidemic. I then partially inspected the
" dwellings of the poor, and have recently completed
" the survey. It is almost incredible that so many
" sources of malaria should exist in a rural district. A
" total absence of all provisions for effectual drainage
" around cottages is the most prominent source of ma-
" laria ; throughout the whole district there is scarcely
" an attempt at it. The refuse vegetable and animal
" matters are also thrown by the cottagers in heaps near
" their dwellings to decompose ; are sometimes not re-
" moved, except at very long intervals; and are always
" permitted to remain sufficiently long to accumulate in
" some quantity. Pigsties are generally near the dwell-
" ings, and are always surrounded by decomposing
" matters. These constitute some of the many sources
" of malaria, and peculiarly deserve attention as being
" easily remedied, and yet, as it were, cherished. The
" effects of malaria are strikingly exemplified in parts of
" this district. There are localities from which fever is
" seldom long absent; and I find spots where the spas-

" modic cholera located itself are also the chosen resorts
" of continued fever."

It appears from the Sanitary Report, from
which I have made the above extracts, and
which was presented to Parliament in 1842,
that there were then 8000 inhabited cellars
at Liverpool; and that the occupants were
estimated at from 35,000 to 40,000. Liverpool is called a prosperous town. People
point with admiration to its docks, and its
warehouses, and speak of its wealth and
grandeur in high terms. But such prosperity,
like the victory of Pyrrhus, is apt to suggest
the idea of ruin. Thirty-five thousand people
living in cellars! Surely such things as these
demonstrate the necessity there is for making
great exertions to provide fit habitations for
the poor. Each year there is required in
Great Britain, according to the Sanitary
Report, an increase of 59,000 new tenements, " a number equal to that of two new
" towns such as Manchester proper, which
" has 32,310 houses, and Birmingham, which
" has 27,268 houses." In these large in-
crements of building, is it not essential that
there should be some care for the health and

the morals of the people? Is it not a question which even in a selfish point of view affects the whole empire?

I am aware that there are great difficulties in the way of any general measure for regulating buildings. The first difficulty which occurs, one which, of itself, forms a limit to building regulations, is, that if you carry them beyond a certain extent, the poorer classes are driven, by the increased expense, from the occupation of cottages to that of rooms, which would be anything but a gain. Besides, it is obvious, on other accounts, that any regulations with respect to building must be introduced with great care, especially in an old country, and where the buildings, which you would be most anxious to modify, are those which will be erected in the immediate vicinity of ground already densely covered with houses. The Liverpool Improvement Act affords a curious instance of, what appears to me, absurd and impatient legislation on the subject of building. By some of its provisions a certain description of cellar in that town will be thrown out of

occupation on a given day. Now, where are
the inhabitants of these cellars to go to ? You
might as well legislate that no food except of
a certain quality should be sold ; but it does
not seem likely that this would secure the
maintenance of the population so legislated
upon. Inconsiderate measures of this kind
occasionally put even wise interference out
of countenance. Still, I must contend that
much good may be done by some simple
building regulations of a sanitary nature.
Much may be done indirectly, all of which
is nearly sure to be good. For instance, it
is very desirable to lower the taxation upon
building materials. Then, again, wherever
the window-tax can be modified, with a view
to benefit the dwellings of the poor, it should
be done. Mr. Biers, a witness examined
before the Select Committee in 1842 on
Building Regulations, says,

" The preamble of this Act (the Bill, I believe, then
" under consideration) sets out that it is for the pur-
" pose of preventing disease and giving better ventila-
" tion ; now, it would much increase the advantages of
" poor people if a rider or addition was made to the
" 17th section, for the purpose of giving a better ventila-
" tion without being liable to the tax-gatherer. I have

" added to this section, ' And, for the purpose of pro-
" moting health and better ventilation, it is provided,
" that all window-lights or casements, not being between
" the outside brick or stone reveals of greater dimensions
" than one foot wide and three feet high, shall not be
" assessed to the window duties, whether the same be
" glazed or not, provided the room or appurtenance is
" not used for a sleeping or dwelling apartment.' "

" *Viscount Sandon.* This is not for inhabited cellars ?
" No, it is to promote the ventilation of any part that
" is not an inhabited room ; larders and cellars and out-
" appurtenances of houses.   I used to put in the build-
" ings I am now erecting what are termed lancet lights,
" for the ventilating the cellars, larders, &c. ; and, pre-
" vious to the late survey, these lancet lights were never
" taken ; but so stringent were the orders from the tax-
" board on the late survey, that if they found a gimlet-
" hole they would take it.

" *Chairman.* Were they glazed ?—Yes.

" If they were not glazed, but made of wire, how
" would that be ?—Then they can take them, unless the
" word ' Dairy' or ' Cheese-room' is written over them ;
" I have now been obliged to reduce three of those lancet
" lights, and do not get the ventilation.   It is as much
" or more concern to the poor than it is to the rich, that
" they should have a proper ventilation ; and there have
" been many windows stopped up (which ought not to
" have been taken) in consequence of the recent survey,
" and which I am sure the Legislature never intended
" should be taken."

But, in addition to these indirect methods for
improving buildings, it is surely not beyond

our legislative ability to devise some very
simple regulations, at least of that kind which
are to have a prospective application. I do
not like to speak confidently about the merits
of the Government Bill, introduced this ses-
sion, because it requires so much technical
knowledge to judge of these matters; but the
main provisions for back-yards or open spaces
attached to dwelling houses, and for the areas
to lowermost rooms, appear to me well considered. This Bill applies only to the metropolis. The working, however, of local
improvement Acts may afford the best kind of
evidence to prepare a general measure upon.
When the subject was considered in Committee in 1842, the Corporation of London
sent a witness who showed that if a certain regulation, embodied in the Bill they were then
considering, were carried into effect, it would,
in some instances, not only injure property,
but prevent improvement. Partial objections of this nature, which after all may be
very slight things, often prevent most useful
measures from being carried. But why should
there not be a discretionary power vested
somewhere to relax any provision which, in

particular cases, might be found harsh or inapplicable? This power might be given to a central office, or to local boards of health. Any suggestion of this kind is liable to objections; and the truth is, that to introduce sanitary provisions into a state of things not prepared for them, must at first be a matter cumbered with difficulties; but, as Lord Lyndhurst has said, " a difficulty is a thing " to be overcome." Mr. Carlyle has pointed out what a wonderful production a soldier is, still more a body of them, and all the apparatus by which they are kept in working order. And, as he goes on to argue, governments could not exist if this human fighting machine were not in good keeping, and, therefore, it is well cared for at all times. Now if governments did but perceive the importance of some regulation for the dwellings of the poor, if they looked at it only as a matter of finance (for, eventually, the state pays for all disease and distress), it is probable they would put their shoulders to the wheel, and get it out of the difficulty, at least as far as their fair share of the matter goes.

Again, the more difficulty there is in legislating on this subject, and especially if it can be shown that there is difficulty connected with it of a kind almost insuperable by mere legislative efforts, the more there remains for private individuals to do. I cannot believe but that human ingenuity, in some form or other, will be able to surmount the evil in question. The difference of expense in building a row of small cottages, back to back, which it will be hard to ventilate, and which must be without the most obvious household requisites, and that of building a row of cottages each of which shall have a yard at the back, will be about 22 per cent. upon the outlay. Where one would cost £100, which is a good price for the lowest class cottages, the other would cost £122. This calculation is independent of the cost of the additional land which would be required. It is melancholy to think that this £22, and the price of the additional land must, in thousands of cases, have determined the health and morality of the inmates. I do not mean to say that this pecuniary difference is a slight matter, but still I do think it is somehow or other to be provided for. There is always this to be

considered, that the better the tenement, the
more it will be cared for. In the same Committee I have mentioned before, the Town
Clerk of Leeds is asked :

" Would not the building of the better kind of cottages
" always secure the best tenants ?—Unquestionably.

" And the person who invested the property in buildings
" of that kind would rather take six per cent. of good
" tenants than seven per cent. of bad ones ?—Yes ; we
" have a number of instances in Leeds. There is a
" gentleman named Croysdill, who has 200 or 300 cot-
" tages ; he receives the lowest rents on an average of
" any large proprietor of cottages, and they are unques-
" tionably the most comfortable dwellings, and the best
" occupied."

It may be a strong thing to say, but I
can conceive it possible, in a Christian country,
for a man to restrain himself from making
the utmost profit out of his possessions. I
can imagine, for instance, an owner of land
in a town being unwilling to demand such a
price for it, as would prevent the cottages of
the. labouring people from being built with
those comforts and conveniences upon which
civilization may almost be said to depend. A
man may think that there is some responsibility attached to ownership; and he may
not like to be in any way accessory to the

building of such habitations for the poor as
he thoroughly disapproves of. And if the
owner of land feels this, still more may the
capitalist who undertakes to build upon it.
It may be a satisfactory thing to collect in
any way much money; but I think, on the
other hand, that most men have a great pleasure in doing anything well, in a workman-
like and stable manner. And, strange as it
may seem, it is very possible that motives of
profit and loss may not be the only ones
which have led to such miserable building,
as is often to be seen in the houses of the
poor. People have not thought about the
matter. If they had seen the merit of building good houses of a small kind, I think that
in many cases, the additional money required
would not have stood in the way. In the
Select Committee of 1842, the following
questions are asked of a witness from Liverpool :

" Is Liverpool a town which has a considerable quan-
" tity of land which may be made available for the pur-
" pose of erecting houses ? — There is a good deal of
" land in the suburbs.

" The corporation possess a good deal of land ?—
" They do.

*   *   *   *   *   *

" Have you had under your consideration the pro-
" visions of what is called Lord Normanby's Act, by
" which it is forbidden to build houses back to back?—
" Yes.

" What were the reasons which induced the Corpora-
" tion of Liverpool not to object to houses being so built?
" —If houses were not to be built back to back there
" would be a great sacrifice of land."

I do not bring this evidence forward to
censure that corporation, but rather to excuse
private persons in some measure, by showing
the general unconcern and ignorance about
the subject. It appears that even a corporate
body, who might be expected to discern the
value of public health and morals, and not to
be subdued by the prospect of immediate and
apparent gain, have at least not made any
endeavour to introduce a good system of
building cottages for the poor of their own
town. Not that they, probably, were in the
slightest degree, more mercenary than other
men; but it is only an instance to show how
little attention has hitherto been given to
this subject.

There is at present in the metropolis, a
Society for " improving the dwellings of the

" industrious classes ;" but what is one society ? This is a matter which ought to interest the owners of property, and the employers of labour, throughout the country.
Such a society as the one named may do great
good by building model houses, making scientific investigations, and frequently laying before the public information on the subject.
But the proper division of labour, as it seems
to me, would be that the state should give
every legislative facility for contemplated improvements in the way of building, should
encourage all researches into the subject, and
be ready to enforce by law such regulations
as, without any great intrusion upon private
property, might secure for small houses those
primary requisites without which it cannot
be expected that they will be anything but
nests of disease. In fact the state might,
eventually, so order the matter that builders
should not merely build such houses as the
poor would take, for there is nothing in the
way of a shelter which they will refuse to
occupy, but such as ought to be let to them,
with due care at least for the public health.
The local authorities should take upon them-

selves, the lighting, cleansing, paving, supplying with water, and the like. For private
individuals there remains the most important
part of the task, namely, the building of an
improved class of small houses. In this good
work the employers of labour may be expected to come prominently forward. Many
a man will speculate in all kinds of remote
undertakings ; and it will never occur to him
that one of the most admirable uses to which
he might put his spare capital, would be to
provide fit dwelling places for the labouring
population around him. He is not asked to
build alms houses. On the contrary, let him
take care to ensure, as far as he can, a good
return for the outlay, in order to avoid what
may, possibly, be an unjust interference with
other men's property ; and also, and chiefly,
that his building for the poor may not end in
an isolated act of benevolence, but may indi-
cate a mode of employing capital likely to
be followed by others. In the present state
of things, the rents of small houses are dispro-
portionately high because of the difficulty and
uncertainty of collecting the rents for them ;
but by any improvement you introduce into

the habits of the occupiers of such houses,
you make this difficulty and uncertainty less;
and thereby diminish rents. And thus, in
this case, as in many others, physical and
moral improvement go on acting and react-
ing upon each other. It is likely, too, that
these poor people will pay with readiness and
punctuality even a higher rent, if it be for a
really good tenement, than a small one for a
place which they must inhabit in the midst
of filth, discomfort, and disease, and therefore with carelessness and penury. Besides,
the rents they pay now, will be found, I believe, sufficient to reimburse the capitalist for
an outlay which would suffice to build tenements of a superior description to the present
ones.

I do not mean to say that the beginners of
such a system of employing capital might
not have a great deal to contend with : and
it is to their benevolence, and not to any
money motives, that I would mainly appeal.
The devout feeling which in former days
raised august cathedrals throughout the land,
might find an employment to the full as religious in building a humble row of cottages,

if they tell of honour to the great Creator, in
care for those whom he has bidden us to care
for, and are thus silently dedicated, as it
were, to His name.

The allotment system has not hitherto, I
believe, been tried to any extent in the manufacturing districts. Mr. James Marshall, and
Mr. Gott, of Leeds have begun to try it; but
I think it is but recently; and that there has
not yet been time to ascertain the result of
the system. I cannot but think, however,
that it will be found more beneficial in manufacturing, than even in rural, districts. Let us
enumerate some of the probable advantages.
It would form an additional means of support—it would tend to endear home to the
working man—it would provide a pleasing
change of employment for him in good times
—it would render him not so listless when out
of work—and it would give him knowledge,
an additional topic of conversation, and an
interest in various things which he might
never, otherwise, have felt the least concern
for. Moreover, it amuses and occupies the
little ones in a family; and it leaves less

temptation for parents to employ children too early, in factories or workshops, when they can find something else for them to do which may be profitable. In this respect, indeed, any improvement in domestic comfort, or any additional domestic pursuit, is likely to be beneficial, as it enlarges the sphere of household duties, and creates more reasons for the wife and children being left at home. Again, as there is hard labour to be done in a garden, this allotment system might occasionally prevent the sense of an almost unnatural dependence being so much exhibited, or felt, when the children are employed in some factory, and the grown up people are not. This is one of the greatest evils that at present attend the state of manufactures. Some of the advantages which I have reckoned above, as likely to be connected with the allotment system, are trifling things; but small impulses, all tending one way, may lead to great results. The main objection which, I suppose, will be taken, is that to make allotments in crowded districts is scarcely practicable. Some beginning, however, has been made at a place so crowded

as Leeds, and at any rate, in any future
building arrangements, room might be left
for allotments of land, which would also secure many advantages with respect to the
sanitary condition of the people. It may be
remarked, too, that any manufacturer, who
possessed cottages with allotments to them,
would have an easy mode of rewarding good
behaviour. Such cottages would be eagerly
sought after by the men, and might be given,
in preference, to those of good character.

Is all this romantic? Is it inevitable that
the suburbs of a manufacturing town must
consist of dense masses of squalid habitations,
unblest by a proper supply of air, light, or
water; undrained, uncleansed, and unswept;
enjoying only that portion of civilization
which the presence of the police declares;
and presenting a scene which the better orders
hurry by with disgust? Or, on the contrary
may we not, without giving ourselves up to
Utopian dreams, imagine that we might
enter the busy resorts of traffic through extensive suburbs consisting of cottages with
their bits of land; and see, as we came along,
symptoms everywhere around of housewifely

occupations, and of homes which their humble owners might often think of with pleasure during their day's labour, looking forward to their return at evening with delight. The richer classes, even those low down in the scale of wealth, mostly struggle to secure some portion of country air for themselves : surely they might do their best to provide for the working man something like a change from the atmosphere of the factory, or workshop, in which he must pass the greatest part of his day throughout the whole year.

Against what I have said above, it may be urged that it would prevent the workman from living near his work. In many cases this may be an inconvenience; but I do not imagine that, in general, it can be proved to be an insurmountable, or even a very serious objection. Turning again to the evidence of the Town Clerk of Leeds before the Building Committee, I find the following :

" *Lord Ashley.* I have been told by several builders
" in London, that in consequence of the improvements
" in the metropolis, great numbers of people have been
" driven to the out-skirts of the town; but they found
" in the out-skirts of the town an excellent house for
" less money than when they lived in miserable lodgings

" in the heart of the town ; is this consistent with your
" experience in Leeds ?—Quite consistent.

" And no hardship to themselves ?—The distance of
" going to work is the objection ; but we find the poor
" people will for twenty years walk two or three miles
" in a morning to their work at six o'clock, and seem no
" worse for it."

V. THE TOWN.

IT will not be a matter unworthy the attention of a great employer of labour, to
improve and embellish the town where his
work is carried on. It is his duty to have
some care for its public buildings, and its
institutions. They are means for improving,
sometimes by manifest benefits, sometimes
by silent influence, the condition of his men.
Surely if the employers of labour felt any
thing like a home affection for the towns
where they live, they could not leave them in
the rude, unadorned state in which so many
of them are. And where is a man's home,
if not where he can do most good ; where he
spends the best part of his life; where he
directs the labour, perhaps, of thousands,
and absolutely by his own exertion may affect

the condition of the rising generation? If
such a man could see the many links of duty
done, or duty disregarded, that connect him
with the spot where he works, let it be ever
so dark, squalid, and repulsive, he would still
say that it was a great part of his home, and
not indulge too fondly in the idea of sunny
meadows and beautiful villas, to be enjoyed
in some secure, golden, retirement. He would
take an interest in the erection of churches,
hospitals, buildings for the display of art, or
indeed, in any institutions that would further
his great work by elevating the sentiments,
or improving the physical condition, of his
men. The establishment of public baths would
be another matter worthy of his attention.
At these baths the poor might be admitted on
payment of a small fee to cover the expense
of attendants. The Romans, induced by
social or political motives, had their public
baths, to which citizens were admitted; who
formed, however, but a small part of their
people: surely higher motives might prevail
with us to have similar baths, which should
be open to all our population. While we
are speaking of institutions of various kinds,

we must not omit Monts de Piété, or Loan
Societies, which may enable the poor man to
get small advances on reasonable terms. It
will not be enough to establish such things
as we have spoken of: there is yet harder
work to be done in the management of them.
All charitable institutions require vigorous
attention; and the better kind of men must
not shrink from the public business which
they are the fittest to transact. If founders
or benefactors were the only people needed,
one generation might monopolize the beneficence of all time; but charitable institutions
require for ever duty to be done by living
men. And, as I have intimated before, it is
in giving thought and labour, that we may
often make the greatest and the most profitable sacrifices for the good of others. But
to go back to mere embellishment—it is
very apt to go hand in hand with material
improvements. Besides, it raises a higher
standard. It declares that there is something besides food and clothing. It may
create, perhaps, the love of beauty and order
in minds that now seem sunk in sense. At
any rate it may do so in a coming generation.

And it is not a little matter if it attach the
wealthier classes to these towns. This naturally brings me to a subject of which I think
the reader will, on consideration, see the importance. I have heard it said, and thought
it a far-seeing remark, that one of the greatest
benefits which could be conferred on manufacturing towns, would be to purify them
from smoke, on the ground that the wealthier
classes would then have less objection to reside in their vicinity: and, especially, that
those who constitute the natural aristocracy
of the place, would not be so much tempted
to remove themselves from the spot where
their fortunes had grown up.

Dr. Cooke Taylor, in his letters to the
Archbishop of Dublin, speaking of the parts
of Manchester which "have been abandoned
" to the poorest grade of all," says,

" Your Grace is aware that to some extent Dublin
" is similarly divided into the city of the rich and the
" city of the poor; but I know that many respectable
" and wealthy manufacturers reside in the liberties of
" Dublin, while the smoke-nuisance drives every body
" from the township of Manchester who can possibly
" find means of renting a house elsewhere."

Now is the doing away of this smoke a sort

of chimerical and Quixotic undertaking ? Not in the least. The experiments appear to be decisive upon this point; and had there been a reasonable care for the health, beauty, and cleanliness of the towns where their work is carried on, the manufacturers would long ago have contrived, I believe, that there should be no such thing as opaque smoke issuing from their chimneys. Count Rumford says in his essays,

" I never view from a distance, as I come into town,
" this black cloud which hangs over London without
" wishing to be able to compute the immense number of
" chaldrons of coals of which it is composed; for could
" this be ascertained, I am persuaded so striking a fact
" would awaken the curiosity, and excite the astonish-
" ment, of all ranks of the inhabitants, and *perhaps* turn
" their minds to an object of economy to which they
" have hitherto paid little attention."

The essay from which this extract is made was published in 1796: what would the Count say now? I believe the calculation which he was thinking of has been made. At any rate a near approximation might be; for I am told, on scientific authority, that " the actual quantity of smoke hanging any " day over London is the fourth part of the fuel

" consumed on that day." Mr. Cubitt, the great builder, in an examination before the House of Commons, quoted by the Sanitary Report, thus expresses himself on this subject :

" With respect to manufactories, here are a great
" number driven by competition to work in the cheapest
" way they can. A man puts up a steam-engine, and
" sends out an immense quantity of smoke ; perhaps he
" creates a great deal of foul and bad gas ; that is all let
" loose. Where his returns are £1000 a month, if he
" would spend £5 a month more, he would make that
" completely harmless ; but he says, ' I am not bound
" to do that,' and therefore he works as cheaply as he
" can, and the public suffer to an extent beyond all cal-
" culation."

To show how little loss is to be apprehended from regulations abating this nuisance, the Sanitary Report cites the authority of

" Mr. Ewart, the Inspector of Machinery to the Ad-
" miralty, residing at Her Majesty's Dock-yard at Wool-
" wich, where the chimney of the manufactory under his
" immediate superintendence, regulated according to his
" directions, offers an example of the little smoke that
" need be occasioned from steam-engine furnaces if care
" be exercised. He states that no peculiar machinery is
" used ; the stoker or fire-keeper is only required to ex-
" ercise care in not throwing on too much coal at once,
" and to open the furnace door in such slight degree

" as to admit occasionally the small proportion of at-
" mospheric air requisite to effect complete combustion.
" Mr. Ewart also states that if the fire be properly
" managed, there will be a saving of fuel. The extent
" of smoke denotes the extent to which the combustion
" is incomplete. The chimney belonging to the manu-
" factory of Mr. Peter Fairbairn, engineer at Leeds, also
" presents an example and a contrast to the chimneys of
" nearly all the other manufactories which overcast that
" town. On each side of it is a chimney belonging to
" another manufactory, pouring out dense clouds of
" smoke; whilst the chimney at Mr. Fairbairn's manu-
" factory presents the appearance of no greater quantity
" of smoke than of some private houses. Mr. Fairbairn
" stated, in answer to inquiries upon this subject, that he
" uses what is called Stanley's feeding machinery, which
" graduates the supply of coal so as to produce nearly
" complete combustion. After the fire is once lighted,
" little remains to the ignorance or the carelessness of
" the stoker. Mr. Fairbairn also states that his con-
" sumption of fuel in his steam-engine furnaces, in com-
" parison with that of his immediate neighbours, is pro-
" portionately less. The engine belonging to the cot-
" ton-mills of Mr. Thomas Ashton, of Hyde, near Stock-
" port, affords to the people of that town an example of
" the extent to which, by a little care, they might be
" relieved of the thick cloud of smoke by which the dis-
" trict is oppressed.

" At a meeting of manufacturers and others, held at
" Leeds, for the suppression of the nuisance of the smoke
" of furnaces, and to discuss the various plans for abating
" it, the resolution was unanimously adopted, 'That in
" the opinion of this meeting the smoke arising from

" steam-engine fires and furnaces can be consumed, and
" that, too, without injury to the boilers, and with a
" saving of fuel.'   Notice of legal proceedings being
" given against Messrs. Meux, the brewers in London,
" for a nuisance arising from the chimneys of two fur-
" naces, they found that by using anthracite coal they
" abated the nuisance to the neighbourhood, and saved
" £200 per annum.   The West Middlesex Water Com-
" pany, by diminishing the smoke of their furnaces saved
" £1000 per annum."

But, putting aside the consideration of any
pecuniary benefit to be gained, I think it
would not be unreasonable to say that no
considerate owner of a factory would wait for
public regulations in this matter, but would,
himself, be anxious to prevent his occupation
from being injurious to his neighbours. In a
manufacturing town, a man may find some
excuse, though a most futile one, in the consideration that it would be of no use for
him alone to consume his smoke, when there
are hundreds of others over whom he has
no influence to persuade them to follow his
example. But you sometimes see one of
these foul-mouthed chimneys blackening a
neighbourhood generally free from such
things, and it does not seem to occur to the

owner of the chimney that he is doing any
thing wrong, provided he is legally secure.
Probably he gives away in the course of the
year such a sum as would put up an apparatus which would modify, if not altogether
remove, the smoke. Let him not think that
charity consists only in giving away something : I doubt whether he can find any work
of benevolence more useful to his neighbourhood and to society in general, than putting
a stop to this nuisance of his own creation.
I am not inclined to rest my case against it
on the ground of health alone; though I believe, with the Sanitary Commissioners, that
it would be found much more injurious than
is generally imagined. When you find that
flowers and shrubs will not endure a certain
atmosphere, it is a very significant hint to
the human creature to remove out of that
neighbourhood. But independently of the
question of health, this nuisance of smoke
may be condemned simply on the ground of
the waste and injury which it occasions. And
what is to be said on the other side? What can
any man allege in its favour? Our ancestors,
who had glimmerings occasionally, held that

" Si homme fait candells deins un vill, per qui il cause
" un noysom sent al inhabitants, uncore ceo nest ascun
" nusans car le needfulness de eux dispensera ové le
" noisomness del smell."   (2 Rolls Abr. 139.)

This is quoted in a grave public document
(the Sanitary Report): had we met with it
elsewhere, we might have concluded that it
came from that chronicle in which Mr. Sidney
Smith found the account which he gives of
the meeting of the clergy at Dordrecht.   I
quote it, however, to show how wisely our
ancestors directed their attention in this instance.   If they had been begrimed with
smoke as we are, and, upon inquiry, had
found that there was no "needfulness" to back
the "noisomeness," it is probable they would
have dealt with it in their most summary
manner.   Whereas I fear that Mr. Mackinnon's "Smoke Prohibition" Bill, amidst
the hubbub of legislation, has great difficulty in finding the attention which it really
deserves.   The truth is, this smoke nuisance
is one of the most curious instances how little
pains men will take to rid themselves from
evils which attack them only indirectly.   If
the pecuniary injury done to the inhabitants

of great towns by smoke could only be put in
the form of a smoke rate, what unwearied
agitation there would be against it.   But
surely we ought not to view with less hostility,
because of its silent noxiousness, a thing
which injures the health of our children, if
not of people of all ages, disfigures our public buildings, creates uncleanliness and gives
an excuse for it, affects in some degree the
spirits of all persons who live under it, renders manufacturing towns less welcome places
of residence for the higher classes (which is
what brings it in connexion with the subject
of this Essay); and is, thereby, peculiarly injurious to the labouring population.   If these
pages should survive to any future age, it will
excite a smile in some curious reader to see
how urgent I have endeavoured to be about
a matter which will then be so obvious—
"What strange barbarous times they must
" have been," he will say to himself: " wis-
" dom of our ancestors, forsooth !"   " Far-off
" reader," if there be such an entity, " do not
" presume: thou hast thy smoke too."

In connexion with the subject of " the

" town," it may be well to go a little into the
matter of sewerage, which almost, above all
things, demands the attention of those who
care for the health of the labouring population, indeed, for the health of rich or poor.

This subject is admirably treated in a section of the Sanitary Report of 1842, under
the head of " Arrangements for public health,
" external to the residences." It is now almost
a trite thing to show how closely connected
imperfect sewerage is with disease. Scientific men will tell you that you may track a
fever along the windings of an open drain.
The Sanitary Report mentions that,

" In the evidence given before the Committee of the
" House of Commons, which received evidence on the
" subject in 1834, one medical witness stated, that of
" all cases of severe typhus that he had seen, eight-
" tenths were either in houses of which the drains from
" the sewers were untrapped, or which, being trapped,
" were situated opposite gully-holes; and he mentioned
" instances where servants sleeping in the lower rooms
" of houses were invariably attacked with fever."

The above is a good instance to show how
necessary it is to have some general measures
on these matters of building and drainage.
The expense of trapping a gully-drain is about

£3 ; at least that is what, I understand, the Commissioners of Sewers are willing to do it for. Now is it likely that any poor man, having one of these nuisances before his door, will go to such an expense to have it prevented. It is probable that it would be very good economy for him to do so, even if his whole savings amounted only to £3. But we all know that few men are far-thinking enough to invest much of their capital in a thing which makes so little show as pure air. What do you find amongst the rich? Go through the great squares, where, in one night, a man will lavish on some entertainment what would almost purify his neighbourhood, and you will often find the same evils there, though in a different degree, that you have met with in the most crowded parts of the town. If the rich and great have so little care about what comes

" Betwixt the wind and their nobility"

you can hardly expect persons, whose perception in such matters is much less nice, to have any care at all. It is evident that the health of towns requires to be watched by scientific men, and improvements constantly urged on by persons who take an especial interest in the subject. If I were a despot, I would soon have a band of Arnotts, Chadwicks, Southwood Smiths, Smiths of Deanston, Joneses, and the like; and one should have gratified a wiser ambition than Augustus if one could say of any great town, Sordidam inveni, purgatam reliqui.

The supply of water is of course one of the chief means for the purification of a town. It is at present, I fear, grievously neglected throughout the country. The Sanitary Report draws attention to the mode of supplying water to Bath, and gas to Manchester: and adduces the latter as an instance "of the practicability of obtaining "supplies for the common benefit of a town "without the agency of private companies." And Mr. Chadwick, after a lengthened investigation into the subject which will well repay perusal, thus concludes:

"I venture to add, as the expression of an opinion "founded on communications from all parts of the "kingdom, that as a highly important sanitary measure "connected with any general building regulations, whe-

" ther for villages or for any class of towns, arrange-
" ments should be made for all houses to be supplied
" with good water, and should be prescribed as being
" as essential to cleanliness and health as the possession
" of a roof or of due space ; that for this purpose, and
" in places where the supplies are not at present satis-
" factory, power should be vested in the most eligible
" local administrative body, which will generally be
" found to be that having charge of cleansing and
" structural arrangements, to procure proper supplies
" for the cleansing of the streets, for sewerage, for pro-
" tection against fires, as well as for domestic use."

It is possible that some of my readers may
think that the wretched state of ventilation,
drainage, and building, which I have been
commenting upon, is mainly to be accounted
for by poverty. It belongs, they may say,
to an old country ; it is the long accumulated
neglect of ages ; it embodies the many vicissitudes of trade which Great Britain has felt;
it is a thing which the people would remedy
for themselves, if you could only give them
more employment and better wages. In answer to this I will refer to an authority
quoted by Mr. Chadwick in his Essay on the
" Pressure and Progress of the Causes of
" Mortality," read before the Statistical Society in 1843.

" In abundance of employment, in high wages, and
" the chief circumstances commonly reputed as elements
" of prosperity of the labouring classes, the city of New
" York is deemed pre-eminent.   I have been favoured
" with a copy of ' *The Annual Report of the Interments*
" *in the City and County of New York for the Year*
" *1842,*' presented to the Common Council by Dr. John
" Griscom, the city inspector, in which it may be seen
" how little those circumstances have hitherto preserved
" large masses of people from physical depression. He has
" stepped out of the routine to examine on the spot the cir-
" cumstances attendant on the mortality which the figures
" represent.   He finds that upwards of 33,000 of the
" population of that city live in cellars, courts, and alleys,
" of which 6618 are dwellers in cellars. 'Many,' he
" states, ' of these back places are so constructed as to
" cut off all circulation of air, the line of houses being
" across the entrance, forming a *cul de sac,* while those in
" which the line is parallel with, and at one side of the
" entrance, are rather more favourably situated, but still
" excluded from any general visitation of air in currents.
" As to the influence of these localities upon the health
" and lives of the inmates, there is, and can be, no dis-
" pute ; but few are aware of the dreadful extent of the
" disease and suffering to be found in them.   In the
" damp, dark, and chilly cellars, fevers, rheumatism,
" contagious and inflammatory disorders, affections of
" the lungs, skin, and eyes, and numerous others, are
" rife, and too often successfully combat the skill of the
" physician and the benevolence of strangers.
" ' I speak now of the influence of the locality merely.
" The degraded habits of life, the degenerate morals, the

" confined and crowded apartments, and insufficient
" food, of those who live in more elevated rooms, com-
" paratively beyond the reach of the exhalations of the
" soil, engender a different train of diseases, sufficiently
" distressing to contemplate; but the addition to all
" these causes of the foul influences of the incessant
" moisture and more confined air of under-ground rooms,
" is productive of evils which humanity cannot regard
" without shuddering.' "

" He gives instances where the cellar population had
" been ravaged by fever, whilst the population occupying
" the upper apartments of the same houses were un-
" touched. In respect to the condition of these places,
" he cites the testimony of a physician, who states that,
" ' frequently in searching for a patient living in the same
" cellar, my attention has been attracted to the place by
" a peculiar and nauseous effluvium issuing from the
" door, indicative of the nature and condition of the
" inmates.' A main cause of this is the filthy external
" state of the dwellings and defective street cleansing and
" defective supplies of water, which, except that no pro-
" vision is made for laying it on the houses of the poorer
" classes, is about to be remedied by a superior public
" provision."

After considering this account of the State
of New York, it will hardly do to say, that,
even under favourable circumstances, you can
leave the great mass of the people to take
care of those structural arrangements with
regard to their habitations, which only the

scientific research of modern times has taught any persons to regard with due attention.

We have now gone over some of the principal places where the employer of labour may find scope for benevolent exertion. It has been a most inartificial division of the subject, but still one that may be retained in the memory, which is a strange creature, not always to be bound by logic, but led along by minute ties of association, among which those of place are very strong and clinging. I now venture to discuss a branch of the subject which can hardly be referred to any particular spot, unless, indeed, I were to name the manufacturer's own house as the fit ground for it: I mean the social intercourse between the employers and the employed. Some persons will, perhaps, be startled at the phrase; hardly, however, those who have come thus far with me. By social intercourse I do not merely mean that which will naturally take place in the ordinary charities, such as visiting the sick, managing clothing societies, and the like: but that intercourse which includes an interchange of thought, an occasional com-

munity of pursuit, and an opportunity of indirect instruction; which may be frequent
and extensive enough to avoid the evil effects
of a sense of perpetual condescension on one
side, and timidity on the other; and which
may give the employer some chance at least
of learning the general wants and wishes of
his people, and also of appreciating their individual characters.

This matter is not an easy one. It requires
tact, patience, discretion, and the application
of several of the maxims mentioned in the
preceding chapter. I am not sure however,
that it is any sacrifice whatever in the way of
pleasure. The manufacturer's family who
occasionally give an evening to social intercourse with their people, will not, perhaps,
find that evening less amusing than many
that they may pass with their equals.

The advantage, to the rising generation of
working people, of some intercourse with
their betters, would be very great. I must
here quote the authority of one who has fully
expressed in action the benevolent views
which he has indicated in the following words.
" No humble cottage youth or maiden will

" ever acquire the charm of pleasing manners
" by rules, or lectures, or sermons, or legisla-
" tion, or any other of those abortive means
" by which we from time to time endeavour
" to change poor human nature, if they are
" not permitted to *see* what they are taught
" they should practise, and to hold intercourse
" with those whose manners are superior to
" their own." This intercourse will probably
lead to something like accomplishments
among the young people. Some of them
will profit more than others from the manners and accomplishments which they will
observe. And such differences will create a
higher order of love among the working people. The manners of one sex will become
different from the manners of the other; and
the difference of individuals in each sex will
be brought into play. All this is favourable
to morality. When people work at the same
kind of work, have no different pursuits to
call out the different qualities of the two
sexes, and have all of them manners of the
same rude stamp, you can hardly expect that
there will be much to ennoble them in their
affections.

But, in themselves, the accomplishments and acquirements, which working people may attain from social intercourse with their betters, are great things. The same kind-hearted employer, whom I have quoted before, speaks thus upon the subject. " Another " point which has appeared to me of great " importance is to provide as many resources " as possible of interest and amusement for " their leisure hours; something to which " they may return with renewed relish when " their daily work is done; which may ren- " der their homes cheerful and happy, and " may afford subjects of thought, conversa- " tion and pursuit among them." Moreover, a habit of attention, and even scientific modes of thought, are often called out in young people when they are learning some game. Besides to do anything, or know anything, which is harmless, is beneficial. A man will not be a worse workman because he can play at cricket, or at chess; or because he is a good draughtsman, or can touch some musical instrument with skill. He is likely to have more self-respect, and to be a better citizen. He cannot succeed in anything without attention and endurance. And these are the qualities which will enable him to behave reasonably in the vicissitudes of trade, or to prepare as much as possible against them.

In the Report on the condition of children and young persons employed in Mines and Manufactures, there is some remarkable evidence given by a man who had himself risen from the state of life which he describes. It leads us to perceive the great good which any improvement in the domestic accomplishments of the women might be expected to produce. He says,

" Children during their childhood toil throughout the
" day, acquiring not the least domestic instruction to fit
" them for wives and mothers. I will name one in-
" stance; and this applies to the general condition of
" females doomed to, and brought up amongst, shop-
" work. My mother worked in a manufactory from a
" very early age. She was clever and industrious; and,
" moreover, she had the reputation of being virtuous.
" She was regarded as an excellent match for a working
" man. She was married early. She became the
" mother of eleven children : I am the eldest. To the
" best of her ability she performed the important duties
" of a wife and mother. She was lamentably deficient
" in domestic knowledge; in that most important of all
" human instruction, how to make the home and the fire-

" side to possess a charm for her husband and children,
" she had never received one single lesson. She had
" children apace. As she recovered from her lying-in,
" so she went to work, the babe being brought to her at
" stated times to receive nourishment. As the family
" increased, so any thing like comfort disappeared alto-
" gether. The power to make home cheerful and com-
" fortable was never given to her. She knew not the
" value of cherishing in my father's mind a love of
" domestic objects. Not one moment's happiness did I
" ever see under my father's roof. All this dismal state
" of things I can distinctly trace to the entire and per-
" fect absence of all training and instruction to my
" mother. He became intemperate; and his intem-
" perance made her necessitous. She made many
" efforts to abstain from shop-work; but her pecuniary
" necessities forced her back into the shop. The family
" was large, and every moment was required at home.
" I have known her, after the close of a hard day's work,
" sit up nearly all night for several nights together wash-
" ing and mending of clothes. My father could have
" no comfort here. These domestic obligations, which
" in a well-regulated house (even in that of a working
" man, where there are prudence and good manage-
" ment) would be done so as not to annoy the husband,
" to my father were a source of annoyance; and he,
" from an ignorant and mistaken notion, sought comfort
" in an alehouse.

" My mother's ignorance of household duties; my
" father's consequent irritability and intemperance; the
" frightful poverty; the constant quarrelling; the per-
" nicious example to my brothers and sisters; the bad
" effect upon the future conduct of my brothers; one

" and all of us being forced out to work so young that
" our feeble earnings would produce only 1*s.* a-week ;
" cold and hunger, and the innumerable sufferings of
" my childhood, crowd upon my mind and overpower
" me. They keep alive a deep anxiety for the emanci-
" pation of the thousands of families in this great town
" and neighbourhood, who are in a similar state of hor-
" rible misery. My own experience tells me that the
" instruction of the females in the work of a house, in
" teaching them to produce cheerfulness and comfort at
" the fireside, would prevent a great amount of misery
" and crime. There would be fewer drunken husbands
" and disobedient children. As a working man, within
" my own observation, female education is disgracefully
" neglected. I attach more importance to it than to any
" thing else."

This evidence is the more significant, because
one sees that the poor woman had the material of character out of which the most engaging qualities might have been formed.
Let her have seen better things in early life,
and even if her schooling had been somewhat deficient, had she but enjoyed the advantage of such social intercourse with her
betters as we are now considering, that poor
woman might have been a source of joy and
hope to her family, instead of a centre of
repulsion.

Dr. Cooke Taylor, in his " Tour in the
Manufacturing Districts," has given a table,

which I subjoin, "showing the degree of instruction, age, and sex, of the persons taken
into custody, summarily convicted, or held
to bail, and tried and convicted, in Manchester, in the year 1841." The table was formed
on statistical details furnished by Sir Charles
Shaw. It shows a state of facts which has
been deduced from other tables of a like
nature, but the facts are of such moment,
that they can hardly be kept too much in
mind; especially when we consider that there
are large towns in which, as I have said
before, half at least of the juvenile population
is growing up without education of any kind
whatever.* If such are the favourable results
even of that small and superficial education,
which by the way I would rather call instruction than education, described in the second
and third headings of the table, what may
we not expect from a training where the youth
or maiden finds in her employers not only
instructors, but friends and occasional com-
panions? What store of labour on the part
of judges, jailors, and policemen, must be
saved by even a few of such employers.

---

* See Appendix.

	TOTAL IN THE YEAR 1841.			DEGREE OF INSTRUCTION.							
				1. Neither Read nor Write.		2. Read only or Read & Write imperfectly.		3. Read and Write well.		4. Superior Instruction.	
	M. & F.	Male.	Fem.	Male.	Fem.	Male.	Fem.	Male.	Fem.	Male.	Fem.
1st Class Taken into Custody	13345	9925	3420	4901	2070	3944	1218	873	119	207	13
2nd Class Summarily Convicted or held to Bail	2138	1661	477	795	265	660	198	193	14	13	..
3rd Class Tried and Convicted	824	645	179	277	100	276	72	82	7	10	..

AGES.

	Under 10 Years of Age.		10 Years, & under 15.		15 Years, & under 20.		20 Years, & under 25.		25 Years, & under 30.		30 Years, & under 40.		40 Years, & under 50.		50 Years, & under 60.		60 Years, & upwards.	
	Male.	Fem.	Male.	Fem.	Male.	Fem.	Male.	Fem.	Male.	Fem.	Male.	Fem.	Male.	Fem.	Male.	Fem.	Male.	Fem.
1st Class	62	6	681	83	1581	656	2425	909	1805	755	1775	582	1018	284	422	85	156	60
2nd Class	4	..	151	17	302	84	418	150	264	93	327	75	129	39	49	14	17	5
3rd Class	..	..	30	2	150	54	196	61	97	21	109	25	43	11	15	3	5	2

Some persons may object to encouraging anything like refinement amongst the operatives; and others, who would hardly object in open terms, find it difficult to reconcile themselves to the idea of it. Whatever there is in this repugnance that arises from any selfish motive should be instantly cast aside. Do not let us be meanly afraid that the classes below us will tread too closely on our heels. What a disgrace it is, if, with our much larger opportunities of leisure, with professions that demand a perpetual exercise of the intellectual faculties, we cannot preserve, on the average, an intellectual superiority fully equivalent to the difference of rank and station. Let the vast tracts now left barren smile with cultivation : the happier lands, which the rivers of civilization have enriched for ages, will still maintain their supremacy. And remember this, that every insight you give the humbler classes into the vast expanse of knowledge, you give them the means of estimating with a deference founded on reason, those persons who do possess knowledge of any kind. Let us have faith that knowledge must in the long run lead to good ; and let us not fancy that our prosperity as a class depends upon the ignorance of those beneath us. Has not our partial enlightenment taught us in some measure to be reconciled to the fact of there being classes above us? And why should we fear that knowledge, which smoothes so many of the rugged things in life, should be found unavailing to soften the inequalities of social distinction? It is the ignorant barbarians who can pluck the Roman Senate by the beard; and who, in the depth of savageness, can see nothing in sex, age, station, or office, to demand their veneration. Make the men around you more rational, more instructed, more helpful, more hopeful creatures if you can; above all things treat them justly: and I think you may put aside any apprehension of disturbing the economy of the various orders of the state. And if it can be *so* disturbed, let it be.

What I have said above is not drawn from airy fancies of my own. Such things as I have suggested, have been done. I could mention one man, who might not, however, thank me for naming him, who has devoted himself to the social improvement of his

working people : and, without such an example, I should never, perhaps, have thought
of, or ventured to put forward, the above
suggestions with respect to the social intercourse between masters and men. It is the
same benevolent manufacturer from whose
letters to Mr. Horner I have made extracts
before. The general system on which he
has acted may be best explained in his own
words. " In all plans for the education of
" the labouring classes my object would be
" *not to raise any individuals among them above*
" *their condition, but to elevate the condition*
" *itself.* For I am not one of those who think
" that the highest ambition of a working man
" should be to rise above the station in which
" Providence has placed him, or that he should
" be taught to believe that because the hum-
" blest, it is therefore the least happy and
" desirable condition of humanity. This is,
" indeed, a very common notion among the
" working classes of the people, and a very
" natural one ; and it has been encouraged by
" many of their superiors, who have interested
" themselves in the cause of popular improve-
" ment, and have undertaken to direct and

" stimulate their exertions. Examples have
" constantly been held up of men who by un-
" usual ability and proficiency in some branch
" of science had raised themselves above the
" condition of their birth, and risen to emi-
" nence and wealth; and these instances have
" been dwelt upon and repeated, in a manner,
" that, whether intentionally or not, produces
" the impression that positive and scientific
" knowledge is the summum bonum of human
" education, and that to rise above our station
" in life should be the great object of our
" exertion. This is not my creed. I am sa-
" tisfied that it is an erroneous one, in *any*
" system of education for *any* class of men.
" Our object ought to be, not to produce a few
" clever individuals, distinguished above their
" fellows by their comparative superiority, but
" to make the great mass of individuals on
" whom we are operating, virtuous, sensible,
" well-informed, and well-bred men." And
again he states that his object is " to show
" to his people and to others, that there is
" nothing in the nature of their employment,
" or in the condition of their humble lot, that
" condemns them to be rough, vulgar, igno-

" rant, miserable, or poor :—that there is
" nothing in either that forbids them to be
" well-bred—well-informed, well-mannered—
" and surrounded by every comfort and en-
" joyment that can make life happy;—in
" short, to ascertain and to prove what the
" condition of this class of people might be
" made—what *it ought to be* made—what is
" the interest of all parties that *it should be*
" made."

Before concluding this chapter, I must say
a few more words on the general subject of
interference. No one can be more averse
than I am to unnecessary interference, or
more ready to perceive the many evils which
attend it. There is, however, the danger of
carrying non-interference into inhumanity.
Mankind are so accustomed to the idea that
government mainly consists in coercion, that
they sometimes find it difficult to consider
interference, even as applied to benevolent
undertakings, and for social government, in
any other than a bad light. But take the rule
of a father, which is the type of all good government, that under which the divine juris-

diction has been graciously expressed to us. Consider how a wise father will act as regards interference. His anxiety will not be to drag his child along, undeviatingly, in the wake of his own experience; but rather, to endue him with that knowledge of the chart and compass, and that habitual observation of the stars, which will enable the child, himself, to steer safely over the great waters. Such a father will not be unreasonably solicitous to assimilate his son's character or purposes to his own. He will not fall into the error of supposing that experience is altogether a transferable commodity. The greatest good which he designs for his son will, perhaps, be that which he can give him indirectly, and which he may never speak to the youth about. He will seek to surround him with good opportunities and favourable means: and even when he interferes more directly, he will endeavour, in the first instance, to lead rather than to compel, so that some room for choice may still be left. Not thinking that his own power, his own dignity, his own advantage are the chief objects for him to look to, his imagination will often be with those whom

he rules; and he will thus be able to look at
his own conduct with their eyes, not with his.
This, alone, will keep him from a multiplicity
of errors. Now the same principles, actuated
by the same kind of love, should be at the
bottom of all social government. I believe
that we shall be better able in practice to
place wise limits to interference by regulating
and enlightening the animus which prompts
it, than by laying down rules for its action
determined upon abstract considerations. The
attempt to fix such rules is not to be despised; but if the persons, or society, about
to interfere on any occasion, desired a good
object from right motives, I think they would
have the best chance of keeping themselves
from using wrong means. In many cases,
an unwise interference takes place from a
partial apprehension of the good to be aimed
at: enlarge and exalt the object; let it not
be one-sided; and probably the mode of at-
taining it will partake largely of the wisdom
shown in the choice of it. If, for instance,
a government saw that it had to encourage,
not only judicious physical arrangements, but
mental and moral development, amongst those

whom it governs, it would be very cautious of suppressing, or interfering with, any good thing which the people would accomplish for themselves. The same with a private individual, an employer of labour for instance, if he values the independence of character and action in those whom he employs, he will be careful in all his benevolent measures, to leave room for their energy to work. What does he want to produce? Something vital, not something mechanical. It is often a deficiency of benevolence, and not an overflow, that makes people interfering in a bad sense. Frequently the same spirit which would make a man a tyrant in government, would make him a busy-body, a meddler, or a pedantic formalist, in the relations of ordinary life. I have taken the instance of father and son, which might be supposed by many as one in which extreme interference was not only justifiable, but requisite. In stating how necessary it is even there to be very careful as regards the extent and mode of interference, I leave my readers to estimate how essential it must be in all other cases where the relation is not of that closely connected character.

I believe that the parental relation will be found the best model on which to form the duties of the employer to the employed; calling, as it does, for active exertion, requiring the most watchful tenderness, and yet limited by the strictest rules of prudence from intrenching on that freedom of thought and action which is necessary for all spontaneous development.

CHAPTER IV.

Sources of Benevolence.

THERE is a common phrase which is likely to become a most powerful antagonist to any arguments that have been put forward in the foregoing pages : and I think it would be good policy for me to commence the attack, and endeavour to expose its weakness in the first instance. If you propose any experiment for remedying an evil, it is nearly sure to be observed that your plan is well enough in theory, but that it is not practical. Under that insidious word " practical" lurk many meanings. People are apt to think that a thing is not practical, unless it *has* been tried, is immediate in its operation, or has some selfish end in view. Many who do not include, either avowedly, or really, the two latter meanings, incline, almost un-

consciously perhaps, to adopt the former,
and think that a plan, of which the effects
are not foreknown, cannot be practical. Every
new thing, from Christianity downwards, has
been suspected, and slighted, by such minds.
All that is greatest in science, art, or song,
has met with a chilling reception from them.
When this apprehensive timidity of theirs is
joined to a cold or selfish spirit, you can at
best expect an Epicurean deportment from
them. Warming themselves in the sun of
their own prosperity, they soothe their con-
sciences by saying how little can be done for
the unfed, shivering, multitude around them.
Such men may think that it is practical wisdom to make life as palatable as it can be,
taking no responsibility that can be avoided,
and shutting out assiduously the consideration of other men's troubles from their minds.
Such, however, is not the wisdom inculcated
in that religion which, as Goethe well says,
is grounded on " Reverence for what is under
" us," and which teaches us " to recognize
" humility and poverty, mockery and despite,
" disgrace and wretchedness, suffering and
" death, as things divine."

There is a class of men utterly different from those above alluded to, who, far from entertaining any Epicurean sentiments, are prone to view with fear the good things of this world. And, indeed, seeing the multiform suffering which is intertwined with every variety of human life, a man in present ease and well-being may naturally feel as if he had not his share of what is hard to be endured. The fanatic may seek a refuge from prosperity, or strive to elevate his own nature, by self-inflicted tortures; but one, who adds wisdom to sensibility, finds in his own well-being an additional motive for benevolent exertions. It is surely bad management when a man does not make a large part of his self-sacrifices subservient to the welfare of his fellow-men. In active life nothing avails more than self-denial; and there its trials are varying and multifarious: but ascetics, by placing their favourite virtue in retirement, made it dwindle down into one form only of self-restraint.

I suppose there are few readers of history who have not occasionally turned from its

pages with disgust, confusion, a craving for
any grounds of disbelief, and a melancholy
darkness of soul. It can hardly be otherwise, when you read, for instance, of the
colossal brutalities of the Roman Emperors,
many of whom indulged in a sportive cruelty
to their fellow men, which reminds one of
children with insects. When you find, again,
some mighty Master of the World, renowned
for valour, and for prudence, one of those
emphatically called the " Good" Emperors,
kindly presenting hundreds of men to kill
each other for the amusement of the Roman
multitude—when you are told that that multitude contained, what may have been for
that age, good men, and gentle women—
when, passing lower down the turbid stream
of the recorded past, you read of Popes and
Cardinals, Inquisitors and Bishops, men who
must have heard from time to time some
portions of the holy words of mercy and of
love, when you find them, I say, counselling
and plotting and executing, the foulest deeds
of blood—when, descending lower still, you
approach those days when law became the
tyrant's favourite scourge, and you find the

legal slave telling his master how he has interrogated some poor wretch " in torture, " before torture, after torture, and between " torture"—when you have some insight into what that thing torture was, by contrasting the hand-writing of the distracted sufferer before and after his examination—when, to your surprise, you read that these very victims of persecution, were themselves restless and dissatisfied, unless they could direct the arm of power against another persecuted race—and when, coming to your own day, you find that men, separated from you by distance, though not by time, can show the utmost recklessness of human life, if differently coloured from their own. Pondering over these things, your heart may well seek comfort in the thought that these tyrants were, or are, rude men, of iron frame, ready to inflict, ready themselves to suffer. It is not so. A Nero clings to his own life with abject solicitude. A Louis the Eleventh, who could keep other men in cages, wearies Heaven with prayers, and Earth with strange devices, to preserve his own grotesque existence. A James the First, who can sanction at the least, if not direct, the torture to be applied to a poor, old, clergyman, was yet in the main a soft-hearted man, can feel most tenderly for a broken limb of any favourite, have an anxious affection for " Steenie and Baby Charles," and an undoubted, and provident, regard for his own " sacred" person. What shall we say, too, of that Chancellor of his, a man, like his master, of a soft heart, full of the widest humanity, and yet, as far as we know, un-conscious of the horror of those ill doings transacted in his own great presence? Why is it that I recall these things? Why do I bring forward what many of us, forgetting the iron weight with which the sentiments of his age press down even upon the mightiest genius, might look upon as a humiliating circumstance far greater than it is, in the life of a man we ought all to love so much? Is history a thing done away with, or is not the past for ever in the present? And is it not but too probable that we ourselves are occa-sionally guilty of things which, for our lights, are as sad aberrations as those which, in read-ing of the past, we have dwelt upon with the profoundest pity, and turned away from in overwhelming amazement? Are we quite sure that none of the vices of tyranny rest with us; and that we individually, or nationally, have not to answer for any carelessness of human life or for any indifference to human suffering?

What is it that has put a stop to many of the obvious atrocities I allude to as disgracing the page of history? The introduction of some great idea, the recognition, probably, in some distinct form of the command " to do " unto others as you would theyshould do " unto you." And this is what is wanted with regard to the relation of the employer and employed. Once let the minds even of a few men be imbued with an ampler view of this relation, and it is scarcely possible to estimate the good that may follow. Around that just idea what civilization may not grow up! You gaze at the lofty cathedral in the midst of narrow streets and squalid buildings, but all welcome to your sight as the places where miserable men first found sanctuary; you pass on and look with pleasur at the rich shops and comfortable dwellings;

and then you find yourself amongst ample streets, stately squares, and the palaces of the great, with their columns and their statues: and if then you turn your thoughts to the complex varieties of modern life, and the progress of civilization and humanity, may you not see the same thing there; how all that is good, and merciful, and holy, is to be traced up to some cathedral truths, at first little understood, just restraining rude men from bloody deeds, and then gradually extending into daily life, being woven into our familiar thoughts, and shedding light, and security, and sanctity, around us? And, as the traveller's first impulse, when he rises in the morning after his journey, is to catch a glimpse of that famous building which must ever be the thing most worthy of note in the city; so, in your travels, would you not look first for these cathedral truths, and delight to recognize their beneficent influence wherever you may meet with anything that is good in man?

And now, reader, I have come to the close of this Essay. I do not assert that I have brought forward any specific, or even any new remedy of a partial nature, for the evils I have enumerated. Indeed I have not feared to reiterate hacknied truths. But you may be sure, that if you do not find yourself recurring again and again to the most ordinary maxims, you do not draw your observations from real life. Oh, if we could but begin by believing and acting upon some of the veriest common places! But it is with pain and grief that we come to understand our first copy-book sentences. As to the facts, too, on which I have grounded my reasonings, they are mostly well known, or might be so; for I have been content to follow other men's steps, and so assist in wearing a pathway for the public mind. I am well aware that I have left untouched many matters bearing closely on the subject, more closely, perhaps, some of my readers will think, than the topics I have taken. In the fields, however, of politics, and political economy, there are many reapers: and the part of the subject which I have chosen seemed to me of sufficient importance to be considered by itself. I know that in much of what I have said, I have

touched with an unpractised hand, upon matters which some of those who are great employers of labour will have examined and
mastered thoroughly. Still, let them remember, that it is one thing to criticise, and another to act. Their very familiarity with the
subject may render them dull to the means
of doing good which their position affords
them. We pass much of our time in thinking what we might do if we were somewhat
different from what we are; and the duties
appropriate to our present position invite our
attention in vain.

To others I may say, there is nothing in
these pages, perhaps, that will exactly point
out the path most fitting for you to take;
still I cannot but think that so many have
been indicated, that you will have no difficulty in finding some one that may lead to
the main object if your heart is set upon it.
If you throw but a mite into the treasury of
good will which ought to exist between the
employers and the employed, you do something towards relieving one of the great burdens of this age, possibly of all ages; you
aid in cementing together the various orders

of the state; you are one of those who anticipate revolutions by doing some little part
of their duty towards the men of their own
time; and, if you want any reward to allure
you on, you will find it in the increased affection towards your fellows which you will always have, when you have endeavoured to
be just to them.

But I would wish to put more solemn
considerations before you. Ask yourself, if
making all allowance for the difference of
times and countries, you think that the payment of poor rates, of itself, fulfils the command to visit the sick, clothe the naked, and
feed the hungry. Depend upon it, our duties,
however they may be varied by the different
circumstances of different periods, cannot be
satisfied by any thing that the state demands
of us, or can do for us. We have each, from
the highest to the lowest, a circle of dependents. We say that Kings are God's Vice-
gerents upon earth : but almost every human
being has at one time or other of his life, a
portion of the happiness of those around him
in his power, which might make him tremble,
if he did but see it in all its fullness. But at

any rate, the relation of master and man is a
matter of manifest and large importance.　It
pervades all societies, and affects the growth
and security of states in the most remarkable
and pregnant manner ; it requires the nicest
care ; gives exercise to the highest moral
qualities ; has a large part in civil life ; a
larger part in domestic life ; and our conduct
in it will surely be no mean portion of the
account which we shall have to render in the
life that is to come.

APPENDIX.

APPENDIX.

ACCORDING to tables of which Mr. Grainger states that he has ascertained the general accuracy, the proportionate numbers among the working-classes in the Birmingham district at present receiving education are as follows :—Out of a population of 180,000 persons,

> 10,902 or 6·05 per cent. attend day or evening schools only ;
>
> 4,141 or 2·30 per cent. attend both day or evening and Sunday-schools ;
>
> 12,616 or 7·01 per cent. attend a Sunday-school only ; making a total of

> 27,659 or 15·36 per cent. of the population attending schools of some kind or other.

Of this number—

> 5,835 are under 5 or above 15 years of age ; leaving
>
> 21,824 children between the ages of 5 and 15 attending school in the borough of Birmingham at the time the schools were visited.

According to the population abstracts of 1821 and 1831, one-fourth of the total population consists of children between these ages. Hence it would appear, that of the 45,000 between the ages of 5 and 15 in the borough of Birmingham—

21,824 or 48·5 per cent. were receiving instruction in
day and Sunday-schools; and

23,176 or 51·5 per cent. were not found receiving instruction in either day or Sunday-schools
within the borough of Birmingham.

(Grainger, Evidence: App. Pt. I., p. *f* 185, l. 13.)

In the Wolverhampton district, including the neighbouring towns of Willenhall, Bilston, Wednesfield,
Sedgley, Darlaston, and also in the towns of Dudley,
Walsall, Wednesbury, and Stourbridge, though there
are many day-schools, yet the chief means relied on for
the education of the working classes are Sunday-schools.
In the Collegiate Church district in the town of Wolverhampton, containing a population of from 16,000 to
20,000 persons, there is no National or British School.
There is not a single school, reading-room, or lending
library attached to any of the manufactories, foundries,
or other works, with one exception near Wednesbury;
there are no evening-schools, and there is only one industrial school in these districts, namely, at Wednesbury.
It is stated in evidence that the great majority of the
children receive no education at all; that not one half
of them go even to the Sunday-schools, and that those
who do go to these schools seldom attend them with re-
gularity. Throughout the whole of these districts, the
proportion that can read is represented as being unusually small; some who stated that they could read,
when examined, were found unable to read a word;
and out of 41 witnesses under eighteen years of age
examined at Darlaston, only four could write their names.
(Horne, Report: App. Pt. II., p. Q 16, ss. 182 *et seq.*)

"The number of children on the books at the different
" schools in Sheffield, comprising every description of
" schools," says Mr. Symons, " was made the subject

" of minute and accurate inquiry in 1838, by the Rev.
" Thomas Sutton, the vicar; and I have reason to be-
" lieve that no material difference has taken place in
" the amount of scholars taught at the 'common' and
" ' middling' private day-schools since Mr. Sutton's
" census was made." From this census it appears that
the maximum number of children on the books of the
different day-schools, including the infant-schools, is
800; but on a personal examination of these schools by
the Sub-Commissioner, he states that a large proportion,
no less than 26.47 per cent. out of the total number on
the books, must be deducted as being continually absent.
" Assuming," therefore, he continues, " that the schools
" thus estimated are a criterion of the rest (and they are
" certainly superior), the number who attend the schools
" out of the 8000 on the books is only 5869. Of the
" number present at the schools visited, when probably
" the least instructed were absent, it appears that 45·83
" per cent. were unable to read fairly, and that 63·43
" per cent. could not write fairly. Taking this as an
" index to the education of the total number on the
" books, it results that, of the whole 8000, 4333 only
" can read fairly, and 2925 only can write fairly, or, in
" other terms, have attained an elemental education."

The population of Sheffield *parish* is computed to be
123,000. Of this number it is assumed that at least
one-fifth will consist of children between the ages of
three and thirteen. There will be therefore 24,600. Of
these more than two-thirds will be of the working classes:
at least 16,500, then, of these classes are of an age at
which they ought to be receiving education at day-
schools; yet little more than one-third of this number,
viz. one only out of 2·8 attend day-schools. It is impossible to ascertain what proportion of those who do

not attend day-schools can read or write; but as it is
certain that they are less instructed by at least one-half,
I have every reason to believe that, out of the total
16,500 working class children, not above 6,500 can read
fairly. Among the older youths there is still less education, for they have had more time to forget the little they
were formerly taught. This estimate is so thoroughly
corroborated by the most trustworthy evidence I have
received, that I entertain the belief that two-thirds of
the working class children and young persons are growing up in a state of ignorance, and are unable to read.
On the books of the Sunday-schools there were during
the last year 2258, of which the average attendance was
only 1708. From this it appears that 24·40 per cent.
or nearly a quarter, are absent of the whole number on
the books of the Sunday-schools. (Report: App. Pt. I.
pp. E 18 *et seq*. ss. 136. 138. 144-148. 150, 151.)

In the returns from the Warrington district it is stated
that nearly three-fourths of the children can read ; but
the Sub-Commissioner reports that of this number nine-
tenths can only give the sound of a few monosyllables ;
that they have just acquired so much knowledge in the
Sunday-schools, and that they will probably attain to
little more during their lives. (Austin, Report: App.
Pt. II. p. M 19, ss. 125 *et seq*.)

*Report on the Physical and Moral Condition of the
Children and young Persons employed in Mines and
Manufactures.*

II.

AN ESSAY

ON THE MEANS OF IMPROVING THE
HEALTH AND
INCREASING THE COMFORT OF THE
LABOURING CLASSES.

THIS Essay is chiefly based on evidence respecting the condition of the labouring classes in towns. It is not, however, necessary, on that account, to consider the subject as applying to those classes only. There is good reason to believe that the state of the agricultural labourers does not differ much, at least in kind, from that of the working people in towns. The remedies for the evils in both are of the same nature; and whatever results are arrived at with respect to the health of towns may generally be adapted, without much difficulty, to the wants of the rural population.

London,
Feb. 6, 1845.

Claims of Labour.

SECOND ESSAY.

CHAP. I.

DISTRESS AMONGST THE LABOURING CLASSES.

KNOWING that there is an element of decay in any over-statement, I was very anxious, in the former Essay, to avoid even the least exaggeration in describing the distressed state of the labouring people. This anxiety was, in that case, needless. An elaborate Report has since been published by the Health of Towns Commission; and the evidence there given more than bears out the statements which I then made.

Indeed, the condition of a large part of the labouring classes, as seen in this Report, is evidently one which endangers the existence amongst them of economy, decency, or morality. You may there see how more than savage is savage life led in a great city. Dr. Southwood Smith in his evidence says,

" The experiment has been long tried on a large scale
" with a dreadful success, affording the demonstration
" that if, from early infancy, you allow human beings to
" live like brutes, you can degrade them down to their
" level, leaving them scarcely more intellect, and no feel-
" ings and affections proper to human minds and hearts."

He mentions that it has happened to him, in his visits to the poor, as Physician to the Eastern Dispensary, to be unable to stay in the room, even to write the prescription.

" What must it be," he adds, " to live in such an
" atmosphere, and to go through the process of disease
" in it?"

In another place he says,

" You cannot in fact cure. As long as the poor re-
" main in the situations which produce their disease, the
" proper remedies for such disease cannot be applied to
" them."

This state of things, too, according to the same authority, is advancing on us:

" Whatever may be the cause, the fact is certain, that " at the present time an epidemic is prevailing, which " lays prostrate the powers of life more rapidly and " completely than any other epidemic that has appeared " for a long series of years."

The experienced student of history, reading of long wars, looks for their consummation in the coming pestilence. Gathering itself up, now from the ravaged territory, now from the beleaguered town, now from the carnage of the battle field, this awful form arises at last in its full strength, and rushing over the world, leaves far behind man's puny efforts at extermination. We have a domestic pestilence, it seems, dwelling with us; and if we look into the causes of that, shall we find less to blame, or less to mourn over, than in the insane wars which are the more acknowledged heralds of this swift destruction? But, to return to detail. Mr. Toynbee, one of the surgeons of the St. George's and the St. James's Dispensary, tells us:

" In the class of patients to our dispensary, nearly all
" the families have but a single room each, and a very
" great number have only one bed to each family. The
" state of things in respect to morals, as well as health,
" I sometimes find to be terrible. I am now attending
" one family, where the father, about 50, the mother
" about the same age, a grown up son about 20, in a
" consumption, and a daughter about 17, who has scro-
" fulous affection of the jaw and throat, for which I am
" attending her, and a child, all sleep in the same bed
" in a room where the father and three or four other men
" work during the day as tailors, and they frequently
" work there late at night with candles. I am also
" treating, at this present time, a woman with paralysis
" of the lower extremities, the wife of the assistant to a
" stable-keeper, whose eldest son, the son by a former
" wife, and a girl of 11 or 12 years of age, all sleep in
" the same bed ! In another case which I am attending
" in one room, there are a man and his wife, a grown up
" daughter, a boy of 16, and a girl of 13 ; the boy has
" scrofulous ulcers in the neck ; the father, though only
" of the age of 49, suffers from extreme debility and a
" broken constitution."

The medical officer of the Whitechapel Union
says,

" I know of few instances where there is more than
" one room to a family."

Mr. Austin, an architect, gives us the following description of Snow's Rents, Westminster, which is but one instance " among many worse," of the state of things produced simply by the want, as he expresses it, of " pro-" per structural arrangement and control."

" This court is of considerable width, upwards of 20 " feet, but the houses are mostly without yards, and the " refuse, when become intolerable inside the houses, is " deposited in the court itself, the whole centre being a " pool of black stagnant filth, that accumulates from time " to time, and is left to decompose and infect the whole " neighbourhood. Ventilation, or rather a healthy state " of the atmosphere is impossible. What little distur-" bance of the air does take place, would appear only " to render its state more intolerable."

Being asked what the condition of this court is with regard to drainage and the supply of water, he says,

" There are none whatever there. In wet weather, " when the water attains a certain height in the court, it " finds its way into an open, black, pestilence-breathing " ditch in a neighbouring court; but in the ordinary " state of things the whole centre of this place is one " mass of wet decomposing filth, that lies undisturbed " for weeks, from which, so dreadful is the effluvia at " times arising, that in the tenants' own words, ' they

" are often ready to faint, it's so bad!' The supply of
" water consists in this: that 16 houses are accommodated
" with one stand pipe in the court! On the principal
" cleaning day, Sunday, the water is on for about five
" minutes, and it is on also for three days in the week
" for one half hour, and so great is the rush to obtain a
" modicum before it is turned off, that perpetual quar-
" relling and disturbance is the result."

If we go now from the Metropolis to some
of the great towns, we find, substantially,
the same account, varied by the special circumstances of each place. Liverpool, which
we will look at next, is probably the worst.
An official enumeration of the court and cellar
population of that town was made two years
ago, from which it appeared that 55,534
persons, more than one-third of the working
classes, inhabited courts; and 20,168 persons lived in cellars. There are also cellars
in the courts containing probably 2000 inhabitants.

" With regard to the *character* of these courts, 629,
" or nearly one-third, were closed at both ends; 875,
" or less than one-half, were open at one end; and only
" 478, or less than one-fourth, open at both ends.

" The cellars are 10 or 12 feet square; generally flag-

" ged,—but frequently having only the bare earth for a
" floor,—and sometimes less than six feet in height.
" There is frequently no window, so that light and air
" can gain access to the cellar only by the door, the top
" of which is often not higher than the level of the street.
" In such cellars, ventilation is out of the question. They
" are of course dark ; and from the defective drainage,
" they are also very generally damp. There is sometimes
" a back-cellar, used as a sleeping apartment, having no
" direct communication with the external atmosphere,
" and deriving its scanty supply of light and air solely
" from the front apartment."

The above extract, and the numbers of the
court and cellar population, are taken from
Dr. Duncan's evidence. He thinks, from extensive data in his possession, that the numbers, as given in this enumeration, are under
the mark. And it is suggested that, possibly,
casual lodgers have been omitted. Dr. Duncan then gives some further details which
enable us more fully to understand what
dog-holes these cellars are.

" Of the entire number of cellars, 1617 have the back
" apartment I have mentioned; while of 5297 whose
" measurements are given, 1771, or one-third, are from
" five to six feet deep,—2324 are from four to five feet,

" and 1202 from three to four feet below the level of the
" street: 5273, or more than five-sixths, have no win-
" dows to the front; and 2429, or about 44 per cent,
" are reported as being either damp or wet."

In cellars of this kind there are sometimes 30
human beings, sometimes more, " furnished,"
as Dr. Duncan tells us, " with a supply of
" air sufficient for the wants of only seven."
Occasionally, in this Report, there are scenes
described in a circumstantial, Dutch-picture
way which the most vigorous imagination,
priding itself on its ingenuity in depicting
wretchedness, would hardly have conceived.
Take the following instance from the evidence
of Mr. Holme of Liverpool.

" Some time ago I visited a poor woman in distress,
" the wife of a labouring man. She had been confined
" only a few days, and herself and infant were lying on
" straw in a vault through the outer cellar, with a clay
" floor, impervious to water. There was no light nor
" ventilation in it, and the air was dreadful. *I had to*
" *walk on bricks across the floor to reach her bed-side,*
" *as the floor itself was flooded with stagnant water.*
" This is by no means an extraordinary case, for I have
" witnessed scenes equally wretched; and it is only
" necessary to go into Crosby-street, Freemason's row,

" and many cross streets out of Vauxhall-road, to find
" hordes of poor creatures living in cellars, which are
" almost as bad and offensive as charnel houses. In
" Freemason's-row I found, about two years ago, a court
" of houses, the floors of which were below the public
" street, and the area of the whole court was a floating
" mass of putrefied animal and vegetable matter, so
" dreadfully offensive that I was obliged to make a pre-
" cipitate retreat. Yet the whole of the houses were in-
" habited !"

Think what materials for every species of comfort and luxury, are perpetually circulating
through Liverpool. If there had not been, for
many a day, a sad neglect of supervision on
the part of the employers, and great improvidence on that of the employed, we should
not see the third part of the working population of such a town immersed in the most
abject wretchedness, and all this wealth passing through and leaving so little of the comforts of life in the active hands through which
it has passed. It may be said, however, that
a considerable part of the population of Liverpool is immigrant, and Irish. Turn then to
Nottingham, or York, or Preston, it is the

same story. Mr. Hawksley, the engineer, says of Nottingham :

" With few exceptions the houses of Nottingham and " its vicinity are laid out either in narrow streets, or more " commonly are built in confined courts and alleys, the " entrance to which is usually through a tunnel from 30 " to 36 inches wide, about 8 feet high, and from 25 to 30 " feet long, so that purification by the direct action of the " air and solar light is in the great majority of these cases " perfectly impracticable. Upwards of 7000 houses are " erected *back to back and side to side*, and are of course " by this injurious arrangement deprived of the means of " adequate ventilation and decent privacy."

Dr. Laycock says of York,

" From these inquiries it appears that in the parish of " St. Dennis, in which strict accuracy was observed, from " 8 to 11 persons slept in one room in $4\frac{1}{2}$ per cent. of the " families resident there; in $7\frac{1}{2}$ per cent. from 6 to 8 " persons slept in one room; of the total 2195 families " visited by the district visitors, 26 per cent. had one " room only for all purposes."

The Rev. Mr. Clay gives an account of an examination of a part of Preston,

" The streets, courts, and yards examined contain about " 422 dwellings, inhabited at the time of the inquiry by " 2400 persons sleeping in 852 beds, i. e. an average of

" 5·68 inhabitants to each house, and 2·8 persons to
" each bed.

" In 84 cases 4 persons slept in the same bed.

"   28 . 5 . . . . .

"   13 . 6 . . . . .

"   3 . 7 . . . . .

"   1 . 8 . . . . .

" And, in addition, a family of 8 on bed stocks covered
" with a little straw."

The results of statistical investigations, with
respect to the duration of life, are in unison
with the inferences that we should naturally
make from the facts before us. Dr. Laycock
shows us that in York, in the best drained
parishes, where the population to the square
rood is 27, and the mean altitude above the sea
in feet is 50, the mean age at death is 35·32; in
intermediate parishes, where the population is
denser and the altitude less, the mean age at
death is 27·29; in the worst drained, worst
ventilated, and lowest situated parishes, the
mean age at death is 22·57. He mentions a
fact well worth noticing, that the cholera in
1832 broke out in the court called " the Hag-
worm's nest," which is in the same spot

where the pestilences of 1551 and 1604 had dwelt. Surely, in these last two hundred years, we might have drained and ventilated a locality which experience had shown to be so attractive to epidemics. The Rev. Mr. Clay has furnished a table, subjoined in the Appendix, showing the progressive diminution of vitality in the respective classes of gentry, tradesmen, and operatives, at Preston. Dr. Duncan says respecting the mortality of Liverpool,

"While in Rodney Street and Abercromby Wards, "with upwards of 30,000 inhabitants, the mortality is "below that of Birmingham—the most favoured in this "respect of the large towns in England—in Vauxhall "Ward, with a nearly equal amount of population, the "mortality exceeds that which prevails in tropical re- "gions. * * * * * 177 persons die annually in "Vauxhall Ward for every 100 dying out of an equal "amount of population in Rodney Street and Aber- "cromby Wards."

Vauxhall Ward is where the greater number of inhabitants dwell in cellars. Well may Dr. Duncan, in commenting on this differ- ence of mortality in Vauxhall Ward and Rodney Street, declare that it is a fact " suffi-

" cient to arouse the attention and stimulate
" the exertions of the most indifferent."

The average age at death in the following
classes is made out from all the deaths which
took place in the Suburban, the Rural, and
the Town districts of Sheffield in the three
years, 1839, 1840, and 1841:

" Gentry, professional persons, and their families   47·21
" Tradesmen and their families   .   .   .   27·18
    " Artisans, Labourers, and their families
" A. Employed in different kinds of trade and
       handicraft common to all places .   .   21·57
" B. Employed in the various descriptions of
      manufacture pursued in Sheffield and its
      neighbourhood .   .   .   .   .   19·34
" Persons whose condition in life is undescribed   15·04
" Paupers in the Workhouse   :   .   .   25·51
" Farmers and their families   .   .   .   37·64
" Agricultural Labourers and their families   .   30·89

In considering such statistics, the premature
death of these poor people is not the saddest
thing which presents itself to us, but the unhealthy, ineffectual, uncared-for, uncaring
life which is the necessary concommitant of
such a rapid rate of mortality.

Since the publication of the preceding Essay, Mr. Pusey's " Poor in Scotland," an abstract which has brought the evidence taken before the Scotch Poor Law Commission within short compass, has been published. This evidence is of a nature that cannot be passed by. We may think that such details are wearisome, but we must listen to them, if we would learn the magnitude of the evil. It is no use proceeding without a sufficient substratum of facts. Turning then to this abstract, we find one minister in Edinburgh saying,

" I visited a part of my parish on Friday last, and in " all the houses I found persons destitute of food, and " completely destitute of fuel; without an article of fur- " niture ; without beds or bedding, the inmates lying on " straw."

Another tells the Commissioners,

" the allowance generally made, is not sufficient to keep " them (the out-door pensioners) in existence at the lowest " possible rate of living."

A third says

" I have often trembled when I have gone at the call
" of duty to visit the receptacles of wretchedness, because
" I felt that I could not relieve the misery which I must
" look upon ; and in such cases, nothing but a sense of
" duty could compel me to go and visit the poor."

And a fourth minister mentions that his poor
parishioners had stated to him

" that they regarded themselves as outcasts from the
" sympathy of their fellow-men."

It also appears from Dr. Alison's evidence
that this distress is increasing. You read of
Glasgow, always fruitful in extreme instances
of misery, that in one of the private poor-
houses, 22 children were found, all afflicted
with fever, and occupying a room *about four-
teen feet square*. The Superintendent of the
Glasgow Police, speaking of a district in the
centre of the town, says

" These places are filled by a population of many thou-
" sands of miserable creatures. The houses in which
" they live are altogether unfit for human beings, and
" every apartment is filled with a promiscuous crowd of
" men, women and children, in a state of filth and misery.
" In many of the houses there is scarcely any ventilation.
" Dunghills lie in the vicinity of the dwellings, and from

" the extremely defective sewerage, filth of every kind
" constantly accumulates."

Touching the immediate object of the en-
quiry, the relief of paupers, we find that Humanity having gone with cold and cautious
steps (giving 4s. a month, sometimes, to
fathers and mothers of families) through the
Southern and middle regions of Scotland,
becomes in the Highlands nearly petrified:
at "the utmost" is only able to divide amongst
" the impotent poor about 3s. 6d. a-head
" for the whole year." I dare say many
things may be urged against this, as against
all other evidence—a bit picked off here,
another pruned off there—this statement modified, that a little explained. Do what you
will: this evidence, like that of the Health of
Towns Commission, remains a sad memorial
of negligence on the part of the governing
and employing classes.

It may be said that the improvidence of
the labouring people themselves is a large
item in the account of the causes of their
distress. I do not contend that it is not, nor

even that it is not the largest; and, indeed, it would be very rash to assert that this class has, alone, been innocent of the causes of its own distress. But whatever part of their improvidence is something in addition to the improvidence of ordinary mortals, belongs, I believe, to their want of education and of guidance. It is, therefore, only putting the matter one step further off, to say that their distress is mainly caused by their improvidence, when so much of their improvidence is the fruit of their unguided ignorance. However true it may be, that moral remedies are the most wanted, we must not forget that such remedies can only be worked out by living men; and that it is to the most educated in heart and mind that we must turn first, to elicit and to spread any moral regeneration. Besides, there is a state of physical degradation, not unfrequent in our lowest classes, where, if moral good were sown, it could hardly be expected to grow, or even to maintain its existence.

The extracts given in the foregoing pages present some of the salient points which these new materials afford of the distressed state of the labouring classes. It is a part of the subject requiring to be dwelt upon; for I believe there are many persons in this country who, however cultivated in other respects, are totally unaware of the condition of that first material of a state, the labouring population, aye even of that portion of it within a few streets of their own residences.

Indeed, everybody is likely at some time or other to have great doubts about this distress which is so much talked of. We walk through the metropolis in the midst of activity and splendour: we go into the country and see there a healthful and happy appearance as we pass briskly along: and we naturally think that there must be great exaggeration in what we have heard about the distressed condition of the people. But we forget that Misery is a most shrinking unobtrusive creature. It cowers out of sight. We may walk

along the great thoroughfares of life without
seeing more than the distorted shadow of it
which mendicancy indicates. A little thought,
however, will soon bring the matter home to
us. It has been remarked of some great
town, that there are as many people living
there in courts and cellars, or at least in the
state of destitution which that mode of life
would represent, as the whole adult male
population of London, above the rank of
labourers, artisans, and tradesmen. Probably we should form the most inadequate
estimate of this court and cellar population,
even after a long sojourn in the town. Now
ponder over the fact. Think of all the persons in London coming within the above
description whom you know by sight. Think
how small a part that is of the class in question, how you pass by throngs of men in that
rank every day without recognizing a single
person. Then reflect that a number of people
as great as the whole of this class may be
found in one town exhausting the dregs of
destitution. When we have once appreciated

the matter rightly, the difficulty of discerning, from casual inspection, the amount of distress, will only seem to us an additional element of misfortune. We shall perceive in this quiescence and obscurity only another cause of regret and another incitement to exertion.

CHAP. II.

REMEDIES AND REFLECTIONS SUGGESTED BY THE HEALTH OF TOWNS REPORT.

HAVING now made ourselves to some extent aware of the distress existing amongst the labouring classes, we will consider the main branches of physical improvement discussed in the Health of Towns Report.

1. VENTILATION.

I PUT this first, being convinced that it is the most essential. It is but recently that any of us have approximated to a right appreciation of the value of pure air. But look for a moment at one of those great forest trees ; and then reflect that all that knotted and gnarled bulk has been mainly formed out of air. We, in our gross conceptions, were wont to think that the fatness of the earth was the tree's chief source of nourishment. But it is not so. In some cases this is almost perceptible to the eye, for we see the towering pine springing from a soil manifestly of the scantiest nutritive power. When we once apprehend how large a constituent part, air is, of bodies inanimate and animate, of our own for instance, we shall be more easily convinced of the danger of living in an impure atmosphere.

And whether it agree with our preconceived notions or not, the evidence on this point is quite conclusive. The volumes of the Health of Towns Report teem with instances of the mischief of insufficient ventilation. It is one body of facts moving in one uniform direction. Dr. Guy noticed that, in a building where there was a communication between the stories, disease increased in regular gradations, floor by floor, as the air was more and more vitiated, the employment of the

men being the same.   But it is needless to
quote instances of what is so evident.   With
respect to the remedies, these are as simple
as the evils to be cured are great.   For instance, there was a lodging house in Glasgow where fever resided; " but by making
" an opening from the top of each room,
" through a channel of communication to an
" air pump, common to all the channels,
" the disease disappeared altogether."   Other
modes of ventilation are suggested in the Report; and one very simple device introduced
by Mr. Toynbee, a perforated zinc plate fixed
in the window-pane furthest from the fire or
the bed, has been found of signal benefit.   I
shall take another opportunity of saying more
upon the subject of ventilation.   Of all the
sanitary remedies, it is the most in our power.
And I am inclined to believe that half per cent.
of the annual outlay of London, that is ten
shillings in every hundred pounds, spent only
for one year in improvements connected with
ventilation, would diminish the sickness of
London by one fourth.

2. Sewerage.

Melancholy as the state of this department is shown to be; destructive annually, I fear, of thousands of lives; it is almost impossible not to be amused at the grotesque absurdity with which it has been managed. One can imagine how Swift might have introduced the subject in Grildrig's conversations with the King of Brobdingnag. " The King " asked me more about our ' dots ' of houses, " as his Majesty was pleased to call them; " and how we removed the scum and filth " from those little ' ant-heaps ' which we " called great towns. I answered that our " custom was to have a long brick tube, " which we called a sewer, in the middle " of our streets, where we kept a sufficient " supply of filth till it fermented, and the " foul air was then distributed by gratings " at short intervals all over the town.* I also

* " There are several thousand gratings which are

" told his Majesty, that to superintend these
" tubes, we chose men not from any par-
" ticular knowledge of the subject, which
" was extremely difficult, but impartially, as
" one may say; and that the opinions of
" these men were final, and the laws by
" which they acted irrevocable. I also added
" that if we had adopted the mode of making
" these tubes which our philosophers would
" have recommended, (but that we were a
" practical people) we might have saved in a
" few years a quarter of a million of our
" golden coins. ' Spangles,' said His Ma-
" jesty, who had lately seen me weighing
" one of the golden likenesses of our be-
" loved Queen against a Brobdingnag spangle
" that had fallen from the dress of some
" maid of honour. Spangles or not, I re-
" plied, they were very dear to us, dearer
" than body and soul to some, so that we

" utterly useless on account of their position, and posi-
" tively injurious from their emanations."—Mr. Dyce
Guthrie.   Health of Towns Report, vol. ii. p. 255.

" were wont to say when a man died, that
" he died ' worth so much,' by which we
" meant so many gold coins or spangles,
" at which His Majesty laughed heartily. I
" then went on to tell the King, of our river
" Thames, that it was wider than His Majesty
" could stride, that we were very proud of
" it, and drank from it, and that all these
" tubes led into it, and their contents were
" washed to and fro by the tide before the
" city; and, then, my good Glumdalclitch
" seeing that I had talked a long time and
" was much wearied, took me up and put
" me into my box and carried me away.
" But not before I had heard the King speak
" of my dear country in a way which gave me
" great pain.   ' Insufferable little wretches,'
" His Majesty was pleased to say, ' as foolish
" when they are living at peace at home as
" when they are going out to kill other little
" creatures abroad,' with more that was like
" this, and not fit for me to repeat."

In sober seriousness, this subject of sewerage has been most absurdly neglected. I

do not blame any particular class or body
of men.   Parliament has been repeatedly applied to in the matter, but nothing has been
done, as it was a subject of no public interest,
though it is probable, if the truth were known,
that in those Sessions in which the subject
was mooted, there were few questions of equal
significance before the House.   There are excellent suggestions in the Health of Towns
Report for improvement in the original construction of sewers, for their ventilation, for
their being flushed, for making the curves at
which the side sewers ought to be connected
with the main trunks, for a better system of
house drainage, respecting which Mr. Dyce
Guthrie has given most valuable evidence, for
the doing away with unnecessary gully drains,
and for conducting all the contents of these
sewers, not into our much loved river, but far
away from the town, where they can do no
mischief, and will be of some use. This is not
a simple matter like ventilation ; and what is
proposed involves large undertakings.   Still
it is of immense and growing importance, and

should be resolutely begun at once, seeing that every day adds to the difficulty which will have to be overcome.

3. Supply of Water.

This is an essential part of any large system of sanitary improvement, and one that does not present very great difficulty. The principal facts which I collect from the Report are, that the expense of transmission is inconsiderable, and consequently that we may have water from a distant source; that the plan of constant supply seems to be the best; that this constant supply, under a high pressure, could be thrown over the highest buildings in case of fire, that it could be used for baths, public fountains, and watering and cleansing streets; that it could be supplied at $1d.$ or $1\frac{1}{2}d.$ a week to the houses of the poor, and for this that they might have any quantity they chose to take. At present the labour of bringing water entirely prevents cleanliness in many of the more squalid parts

of the town : and the advantage of a constant
and unlimited supply would be almost incal-
culable.   There appears to be some difficulty
in applying the principle of competition to
the supply of water ; for the multiplication
of water companies has in some instances
only produced mischief to the public.   I
would suggest to the political economist
whether there may not be some spheres too
limited for competition.   But these are questions which I cannot afford at present to
dwell upon.

4. BUILDING OF HOUSES.

IN considering this branch of the subject,
the first thing that occurs is the absolute
necessity of getting sufficient space to build
upon.   Other improvements may follow ; but
almost all of them will be defective, if this
primary requisite be wanting.   Hence it is of
such importance to combat the notion that
people must live near their work.   It is a great
convenience, no doubt.   But the question is

not of living near their work, but of dying, or being perpetually ill, near it. Mr. Holland has made a calculation from which it appears, that in some parts of the town of Chorlton-upon-Medlock, in a family of five individuals, " there will be on the average " about 50 days a year more sickness *due to* " *the insalubrity of the dwellings.*" To avoid this additional illness, it is surely worth while for working men to live even at a considerable distance from their work. Indeed I think two or three miles is not such a distance as should prevent them. Besides, is it not probable that, in many instances, the work would come to them?

Supposing that new building takes place, whether from the poorer classes tending more to the suburban districts, or from the dense parts of towns being rebuilt, much might be done by modifying, if not repealing, the window tax and the tax on bricks.

With respect to the next point, the laying out of the ground, there are most valuable suggestions given by Mr. Austin in the Health of

Towns Report. The result of his evidence is, that the average rental paid now in Snow's Fields, a place which I have endeavoured to make the reader acquainted with before, would return upwards of 10 per cent. upon money laid out in making a substantial set of buildings to occupy the place of the present hovels; and that these new houses should have " every structural arrangement " requisite to render them healthy and com- " fortable dwellings." I have only to add on this subject, that it would be of the utmost advantage in any new buildings, and especially for small houses, likely to be built by small capitalists, that there should be a survey made of every town, and its suburbs, with ' contours of equal altitude.'* As things

---

* " To give an idea of the principle of contour lines, " we may suppose a hill, or any elevation of land covered " with water, and that we want to trace the course of all " the levels at every 4 feet of vertical height; suppose " the water to subside 4 feet at a time, and that at each " subsidence the line of the water's edge is marked on

are managed at present, people building without any reference to a general scale, or any
connexion with each other (the non-interference principle carried to its utmost length)
the greatest difficulties in the way of sanitary
improvement are introduced where there need
have been none.

The main branches of sanitary improvement touched upon by the Report are enumerated above. There are, however, some
general results and principles which demand
our especial attention.

In the first place it seems to be universally
true that economy goes hand in hand with
sanitary improvement. So beneficently is the
physical world constructed, that our labour

" the hill; when all the water is withdrawn, supposing
" the hill to be 24 feet high, it will be marked with a set
" of six lines, denoting the contours of each of the levels,
" exactly 4 feet above each other."—Mr. Butler Williams's evidence before the Health of Towns Commission.

for sanitary ends is eminently productive. The order of Providence points out that men should live in cleanliness and comfort which we laboriously and expensively contravene. In the Appendix I subjoin a table drawn up by Mr. Clay, showing in detail the saving produced by sanitary measures. I may notice, as bearing on the point of economy, that there is concurrent evidence showing an excessive rate of mortality to be accompanied by excessive reproduction. Consequently, the result of the present defective state of sanitary arrangements is, that a disproportionate number of sickly and helpless persons of all ages, but chiefly children, are thrown upon the state to be provided for. If this were to occur in a small community it would be fatal. In a great state it is not more felt than a calamitous war, or an adverse commercial treaty. But it requires a continued attention as great as that which those more noisy calamities are able to ensure for themselves while they are in immediate agitation.

Secondly, it is stated that the seats of disease are the seats of crime, a result that we should naturally expect.

Again, it appears from many instances that what we are wont to call the improvements in great towns are apt to be attended by an increase of discomfort to the poor. To them, the opening of thoroughfares through densely crowded districts, in the displacement which it creates, is an immediate aggravation of distress. Considering this, ought we not to endeavour that improvements for the rich and the poor should go on simultaneously? It is a hard measure to destroy any considerable quantity of house property appropriated to the working classes, and thereby to raise their rents and densify their population, without making any attempt to supply the vacuum thus created in that market.

It is stated by Dr. Arnott " that nearly " half of the accidental illnesses that occur

" among the lower classes might be prevented
" by proper public management:" a statement which the general body of evidence, I
think, confirms. Now, consider this result.
Think what one night of high fever is: then
think that numbers around you are nightly
suffering this, from causes which the most
simple sanitary regulations would obviate
at once. When you are wearied with statistical details, vexed with the difficulty of
trying to make men do any thing for themselves, disgusted with demagogues playing
upon the wretchedness of the poor, then
think of some such signal fact as this; and
you will cheerfully, again, gird up yourself
to fight, as heretofore, against evils which
are not to be conquered without many kinds
of endurance as well as many forms of endeavour.

I do not wish to raise a senseless moan
over human suffering. Pain is to be borne
stoutly, nor always looked on with unfriendly
eye. But surely we need not create it in
this wholesale fashion; and then say that

that which is a warning and a penalty, is but wholesome discipline, to be regarded with Mussulma n indifference.

I come now to what seems to me the most important result obtained in the whole course of the elaborate evidence taken before the Health of Towns Commission. It appears not only that distress can exist with a high rate of wages, without apparently any fault on the part of the sufferers ;* but, actually, that in some instances, *there is an increase of sickness with an increase of wages.*† The medical officer of the Spitalfields' District states that the weavers have generally less fever when they are out of work. This statement is confirmed by testimony of a like nature from Paisley, Glasgow, and Manchester. It is one of the most significant facts

---

* See Mr. Toynbee's Evidence. Health of Towns Report, vol. i. pp. 87, 88.

† See Dr. Arnott's Evidence. Health of Towns Report, vol. i. pp. 45, 46.

that has struggled into upper air.   We talk
of the increase of the wealth of nations—it
may be attended by an increase of misery
and mortality, and the production of additional thousands of unhealthy, parentless,
neglected human beings.   It may only lead
to a larger growth of human weeds.   The
explanation of the matter is simple.   Dr.
Southwood Smith tells us that " Fever is the
" disease of adolescence and manhood."
Now, wretched as the dwelling houses of the
poor are, *their places of work are frequently
still worse.** Consequently, with an increase
of work, there comes an increase of fever
from working in ill-ventilated rooms, an
increase of poor-rates,† and an especial increase of orphanage and widowhood, as the
fever chiefly seizes upon persons in the prime
of life.   And a large part of this increase is

---

* See Dr. Guy's Evidence.   Health of Towns Report,
vol. i. p. 92.

† In St. George's, Southwark, out of 1467 persons
who received parochial relief, 1276 are reported to have
been ill with fever.

thus distinctly brought home to neglect, or ignorance, on the part of the employers of labour. Surely, as soon as they are made cognizant of this matter, they will at once hasten to correct it. In the appendix to this work there is a letter from Dr. Arnott, giving an account of the causes of defective ventilation, and the remedies for it. We can no longer say that the evil is one which requires more knowledge than we possess to master it. Science, which cannot hitherto be said to have done much for the poor, now comes to render them signal service. It is for us to use the knowledge, thus adapted to our hands, for a purpose which Bacon describes as one of the highest ends of all knowledge, " the relief of man's estate." Consider the awful possibility that we may at some future time fully appreciate the results of our doings upon earth. Imagine an employer of labour having before him, in one picture as it were, groups of wretched beings, followed by a still more deteriorated race, with their vices and their sufferings expressed in some material, pal-

pable form—all his own handiwork in it
brought out—and at the end, to console him,
some heaps of money. If he had but a
vision of these things by night, while yet on
earth, such an all-embracing vision as comes
upon a drowning man! Then imagine him to
awake to life. You would not then find that
he knew methods of ensuring to his workmen
fresh air, but lacked energy, or care, to adventure any thing for them. Talk not to me
of money, he would say—Money-making
may be one of the conditions of continuance
in this matter that I have taken in hand,
but on no account the one great object.
Indeed, if a man cannot make some good
fabric by good means, he would perform a
nobler part, as Mr. Carlyle would tell us, in
retiring from the contest, and saying at once
that the nature of things is too hard for him.
He is far, far, better conquered in that way,
than obstructing the road by work badly
done, or adding to the world's difficulties by
inhumanity.

What I have given is but an outline of the Health of Towns Report; and I would fain persuade my readers to turn to the original itself. Some delight in harrowing tales of fiction : here are scenes indicated, if not absolutely depicted, which may exercise the tenderest sympathies. Others are ever bending over the pages of history : here, in these descriptions of the life of the poor, are sources of information respecting the well-being of nations, which history, much given to tell only of the doings of the great, has been strangely silent upon. For the man of science, for the moral philosopher, or even for the curious observer of the ways of the world, this Report is full of interesting materials. But it is not as a source of pleasurable emotion that our attention should be called to it. It is because without the study of such works, we cannot be sure of doing good in the matter. If there is anything that requires thought and experience, it is the exercise of Charity in such a complicated system as modern life. Indeed, there is scarcely anything to be done wisely in it without knowledge. And I believe it would be better, for instance, that people should read this Health of Towns Report, than that they should subscribe liberally to carrying out even those suggestions which are recommended by men who have thought upon these subjects. There is no end to the quickening power of knowledge; but mere individual, rootless acts of benevolence are soon added up.

There is not the less necessity for this knowledge, because public attention is in some measure awakened to the duties of the employers of labour. I do not know a more alarming sight than a number of people rushing to be benevolent without thought. In any general impulse, there are at least as many thoughtless as wise persons excited by it : the latter may be saved from doing very foolish things by an instinct of sagacity; but for the great mass of mankind, the facts require to be clearly stated and the inferences carefully drawn for them, if they are to be prevented from wasting their benevolent impulses upon foolish or mischievous undertakings.

CHAP. III.

By what Means the Remedies may be effected.

CERTAINLY, whether built upon sufficient information or not, there is at the
present time a strong feeling that something
must be done to improve the condition of the
labouring classes. The question is, how to
direct this feeling—where to urge, where to
restrain it; and to what to limit its exertions.
An inane desire for originality in such matters
is wholly to be discouraged. People must not
dislike taking up what others have begun.
Of the various modes of improving the sanitary condition of the labouring classes, each
has some peculiar claim. Ventilation is so
easy, and at the same time so effective, that

it seems a pity not to begin at once upon
that. Again, structural arrangements connected with the sewerage of great towns are
pressing matters, because, like the purchase
of the Sybil's books, you have less for your
money, the longer you delay. These two
things and the supply of water seem to me the
first points to be attacked; but a prudent
man will endeavour to fall in with what others
are doing, if it coincides with his direction,
and he can thereby hasten on, not exactly
his own methods, but the main result which
he has in hand.

There is one conclusion which most persons
who have thought on these subjects seem
inclined to come to—namely, that a Department of Public Health is imperatively wanted,
as the duties to be performed in this respect
are greater than can be thrown upon the
Home Secretary. I venture to suggest one
or two things which it might be well to consider in the formation of such a Department.
It should not be a mere Medical Board under
one of the great branches of the Executive;

but an entirely independent Department. It will thus have a much firmer voice in Parliament, and elsewhere. Scientific knowledge, as well as legal and medical, should be at its daily command. I lay much stress upon the first, and for this reason. Medical men, who are not especially scientific, are apt, I suspect, to be " shut up in measureless con-" tent" with the old ways of going on. Their knowledge becomes stereotyped. And as, in such a Department, the aid of the latest discoveries is wanted, it is better to rely upon those whose especial business it is to be acquainted with them. All departments and institutions are liable to become hardened, and to lose their elasticity. It is particularly desirable that this should be avoided in a Department for the Public Health ; and, therefore, great care should be taken in the constitution of it, to ensure sufficient vitality, and admit sufficient variety of opinion, or it would be better to trust to getting each special work done by new hands. The change of political chiefs, a thing frequent enough in

modern times, will ensure some of that diver-
sity of mind which is one of the main inducements for lodging power in a Commission
or a Board.

It is a great question what authority should
be entrusted by this central body to Munici-
palities or local bodies. They should certainly
have the utmost that can discreetly be given
to them. It does not do to say that, hitherto,
they have been totally blind to their duty in
this matter. So have other people been. The
great principle of an admixture of centrali-
zation with local authority should not be lost
sight of without urgent reasons. That any
reform should be undertaken in sanitary
measures betokens an improved state of moral
feeling. The feeling amongst the most influential classes which produces the legislative
reform may be expected to go lower down—
indeed, the reform has already, in all proba-
bility, found some of its most useful supporters in a lower class—and therefore we
may expect to find fit persons to work in
the lower executive departments. It is not

fair to go back and assume that the old state of feeling exists—in fact, that the parchment law is changed, and not the people. This might be so in a despotic government, but not here. It is an oversight, when, in such cases, a general improvement is not calculated upon.

One of the first things that might be attempted in the legislative way is Smoke Prohibition. It is exactly a matter for the interference of the state. The Athenian in the comedy, wearied of war, concludes a separate peace with the enemy for himself, his wife, his children, and his servant; and forthwith raises a jovial stave to Bacchus. Now all sensible people would not only be glad to enter into amicable relations with Smoke, but would even be content to pay a good sum for protection against the incursions from factory chimnies and other nuisances in their neighbourhood. But there is no possibility of making such private treaties. The common undistinguishable air is vitiated : and we ask the State, for the sake of the common

weal, to see this matter righted. It has been
long before the public; and there is sufficient
evidence to legislate at once upon. At any
rate, if Mr. Mackinnon's bill is referred to a
Committee, it ought to be upon the understanding that the suggestions of the Committee shall be forthwith and earnestly considered, with a view to instant legislation.
If the Committee were to make an excursion
into the smoke-manufacturing parts of the
Metropolis, they would see here and there
factory chimnies from which less smoke issues
than from private houses. This seems to be
conclusive. They will not find, I think, that
these smokeless chimnies belong to unimportant factories. Now, if the nuisance can be
cured in one case, why not in all? Here we have
new and stately public buildings, in the East
and the West of the town, which only a few
of us, for a short time, will see in their pristine
purity. If we cannot appreciate the mischief
which this smoke does to ourselves, let us have
some regard for the public buildings. Consider, too, at what an immense outlay we pur-

chase this canopy of smoke. Certainly at hundreds of thousands a year in London alone. We have, therefore, made an investment in smoke of some millions of money. If we had but the resources to spend upon public improvements, which have thus been worse than wasted, we should need no other contribution. Moreover, the proposed restrictions in the case of smoke would not only be beneficial to the public, but profitable to the individual: and the more one considers the subject, the more astonished one is, that they should not long ago have been enacted.

But the truth is, we are quite callous to nuisances. A public prosecutor of nuisances is more wanted than a public prosecutor of crime. And this is one of the things that would naturally come under the supervision of a Department of Health. I find, from the Health of Towns Report, that it is proposed to permit the continuance of sundry noxious trades in London for thirty years, and then they are to be carried on under certain restrictions. It cannot be said that

this is selfish legislation : the present generation may inhale its fill of gas and vitriol;
but our grandchildren will imbibe " under
certain restrictions" only that quantity which
is requisite to balance the pleasures of a
city life. At Lyons there is a long line
of huge stumps of trees bordering on the
river. The traveller, naturally enough, sup-
poses that this is the record of some civil
commotion ; but, on inquiry, he finds that the
fumes of an adjacent vitriol manufactory have
in their silent way levelled these magnificent
trees as completely as if it had been done by
the most effective cannonade. If we could
but see in some such palpable manner how
many human beings are stunted by these
nuisances, we should proceed in their expul-
sion with somewhat of the vigour which it
deserves. Imagine, if only for one day, we
could enjoy a more than lynx-like faculty,
and could see, not merely through rocks,
but into air, what an impressive sight it
would be in this Metropolis. Here, a heavy
layer of carbonic acid gas from our chim-

nies—there, an uprising of sulphuretted hydrogen from our drains—and the noxious breath of many factories visible in all its varieties of emanation. After one such insight, we should need no more Sanitary Reports to stimulate our exertions. But it is only our want of imagination that prevents us from apprehending now the state of the atmosphere. Science demonstrates the presence of all that I have pictured, and far more.

Great resistance might, perhaps, be made, if large measures were to be taken for the removal of noxious trades from great towns. In many cases, where rapid measures would be harsh and unjust, it would be well worth while for the community to buy the absence of these unpleasant neighbours, resolutely shutting the gates against the incoming of any similar nuisances for the future. On the other hand, mere clamour about the rights of property and the injustice of interference must be firmly resisted. This clamour has been made in all times. Indeed, men seldom raise a more indignant outcry than when they are prevented from doing some injury to their neighbours. How the feudal barons must have chafed, when deprived of the right of hanging in their own baronies : how cruel it doubtless seemed to the monopolists of olden times, when some " factious" House of Commons summoned to its bar the Sir Giles Overreaches, and made them disgorge their plunder : how planters in all climes storm, if you but touch the question of loosening the fetters of their slaves. And so, in these minor matters, when the community, at last awake to its interest, forbids some injurious practice to go on any longer, it is natural that those who have profited by it, and who, blinded by self-interest, still share the former inertness of the public, should find it hard to submit quietly and good-naturedly to have any restrictive regulations put upon their callings. And where the public can smooth this in any way, they ought to do so ; not grudging even large outlay, so that the nuisances in question be speedily and effectually removed. The money spent by the community on sanitary purposes is likely to be the most reproductive part of its expenditure, and especially beneficial to the poorer classes who, for the most part, live near these nuisances, and have few means of resisting their noxious influence.

After discussing what might be done by legislation, we come naturally to consider what might be done by Associations for benevolent purposes. However inadequate such Associations may be as an equivalent for individual exertion, there are, doubtless, many occasions on which they may come in most effectively; doing that which individuals can hardly undertake. In London, for instance, an association that would give us an elaborate Survey of the town, would accomplish a most benevolent purpose, and not be in any danger of interfering unwisely with social relations. The same may be said of our other towns, for, I believe, there is not one of them possessing a Survey fit to be used for building and sanitary improvements. Again, there are certain fields at Battersea at present unbuilt upon, close to the river, one of those spots near the metropolis that ought to be secured at once for purposes of public health and amusement: if a Society will do that for us, they will accomplish a noble work. Happily, the necessity for public parks is beginning to be appreciated. These are the fortifications which we should make about our towns. Would that, on every side of the Metropolis, we could see such scenes as this so touchingly described by Goethe.

" Turn round, and from this height look back upon
" The town: from its black dungeon gate forth pours,
" In thousand parties, the gay multitude,
" All happy, all indulging in the sunshine!
" All celebrating the Lord's resurrection,
" And in themselves exhibiting, as 'twere
" A resurrection too—so changed are they,
" So raised above themselves. From chambers damp
" Of poor mean houses—from consuming toil
" Laborious—from the work-yard and the shop—
" From the imprisonment of walls and roofs,
" And the oppression of confining streets,
" And from the solemn twilight of dim churches—
" All are abroad—all happy in the sun."

Anster's Faust.

Many other excellent enterprises might be suggested which societies are peculiarly fitted to undertake. I must own that I think they are best occupied in such matters as will not require perpetual looking after, which when they are once done are wholly done, such as the formation of a park, the making of a survey, the collection of materials for a legislative measure, and the like. These bodies are called in for an exigency, and we should be able to contemplate a time when their functions will cease ; or at least when their main work will be done.

Other limits in their choice of objects might be suggested. For instance, it is desirable that they should address themselves, in preference, to such purposes as may benefit people indirectly; or such as concern the public as a body rather than distressed individuals of the public; or that aim at supplying wants which the people benefited are not likely in the first instance to estimate themselves. Such is the supply of air, light, and the means of cleanliness. There is small danger of corrupting industry by giving any extent of facilities for washing.*

While we are on this subject, we must not pass over the societies which have started up in connexion with our immediate object. These " Baths and Washhouses for the Poor" are an admirable charity, obvious to very little of the danger which is apt to threaten benevolent undertakings. It would, how-

---

* The mischief that may be done by associations for benevolent purposes, when ill-directed, is admirably shown in a pamphlet on the subject of Visiting Societies by " Presbyter Catholicus." James Darling, Little Queen Street, 1844. One of the objects of this pamphlet is to show that the command addressed to alms-givers " not to let their left hand know what their right " hand doeth," concerns the receiver as much as the giver—that " a man's alms will be converted into a " source of almost unmixed evil, if their distribution " become a subject of notoriety," which is the case in public charities. This, like most general propositions, is not to be construed over strictly; but there is much truth in it, (especially if we take the word " alms " in its most restricted sense) and it deserves to be weighed carefully by all who wish to render their benevolence most available.

ever, be a most serious drawback on their utility, if they were to render people indifferent to the much greater scheme of giving a constant supply of water at home. With respect to the building associations for the improvement of the houses of the poor, their efforts, as it seems to me, will be most advantageously directed, not in building houses, but in buying and preparing ground, and letting it out to the individual builder upon conditions compelling the desired structural arrangements. In this way they may immensely extend the sphere of their usefulness. It is not by limiting their profit, and so insisting upon proving their benevolence, but by giving birth to the greatest amount of beneficial exertion on the part of individuals, that they may do most good.

We come now to consider what may be done by individual exertion. Here it is, that by far the largest field is open for endeavour: here, that neglect is most injurious. Many a man who subscribes largely to charities, has created more objects for them, than he has furnished them with means to relieve, if he has neglected but a little his duties as an employer of labour, or an owner of property. This mischief arises from considering charity as something separated from the rest of our transactions; whereas a wise man weaves it in with them, and finds the first exercise for it in matters that grow out of his nearest social relations, as parent, master of a household, employer of labour, and the like.

The more we look into the question, the more weight, I think, we shall attach to individual exertion. Take it in all its branches. Consider the most remarkable impulse ever given to the energies of Europe—the Crusades. It was an aggregate of individual impulses. Every strong and enterprising man felt that it was a matter which concerned his own soul. It was not only that he was to cause something to be done for the great object, but, if possible, he was to do it himself. A Crusade against Misery is called for now; and it will only be carried on successfully by there being many persons who are ready to throw their own life and energy into the enterprise. Mere mercenary aid alone will never do it.

Look, moreover, at what one man can do. A Chatham springs into power, and we are told that down to the lowest depths of office a pulsation is felt which shows that there is a heart once more at the summit of affairs. The distant sentinel walks with a firmer tread on the banks of the Ebro, having heard that the Duke has arrived at head quarters. So, throughout. Every where you find individual energy the sustaining power. See, in public offices, how it is the two or three efficient men who carry on the business. It is when some individuals subscribe largely in time, thought, and energy, to any benevolent association that it is most like to prosper —for then it most resembles one powerful devoted man. The adding up of many men's indolence will not do. You think, perhaps, listless man of rank or wealth, that your order sustains you. Short time would it do so, but for the worthy individuals who belong to it, and who, at the full length of the lever, are able to sustain a weight which would throw the worthless, weightless men into air in a minute.

In the above cases it has been one man wielding much power ; but in the efforts that are wanted to arrest the evils which we have been considering, the humblest amongst us has a large sphere of action. A provident labouring man, for example, is a blessing to his family and to his neighbours ; and is thus doing what he best can, to relieve even national distress.

It is a total mistake to bring, as it were, all the misery and misfortune together, and say, now find me a remedy large as the evil, to meet it. Resolve the evil into its original component parts. Imagine that there had been no such thing as the squandering, drinking, absentee Irish landlords we read of in the last generation—do you suppose that we should have as many inhabitants

in St. Giles's, and the Liverpool cellars, to
look after now? So, with the English landlords and manufacturers of that time, see what
a subtraction from the general mass of difficult
material there would have been, if those men
had done their duty. But you will say we are
still talking of bodies. Imagine, then, that
during the last generation there had been the
energetic efforts of individuals in these bodies,
that there are now, directed to the welfare of
the people under them. It would, no doubt,
have been a great easement of the present
difficulty. Any body who does his duty to
his dependents keeps a certain number out of
the vortex; and his example is nearly sure to
be followed, if he acts in an inoffensive,
modest fashion. Dr. Arnott has shown what
great things may be done in the way of ventilation by individual employers. See what
benefit would arise if only some few builders,
taking to heart the present miserable accommodation for the poor, which few know
better than they do, would, in their building
enterprises, speculate also in houses of the

smaller kind, and take a pride in doing the utmost for them.

One might easily multiply instances where individual exertion would come in ; but each man must in some measure find out the fit sphere of action for him.   " The States-" man" tells us that the real wealth of a state is the number of " serviceable" minds in it.   The object of a good citizen should be to make himself part of this wealth.   Let him aid where he can in benevolent associations, if well assured of their utility, and at the same time mindful of the duty of private endeavour; but do not let him think that he is to wait for the State's interference, or for co-operation of any kind.   I do not say that such aids are to be despised, but that they are not to be waited for, and that the means of social improvement are in every body's hands.   For warfare, men are formed in masses, and scientific arrangement is the soul of their proceedings.   But industrial conquests and, especially, the conquests of benevolence, are often made, here somewhat

and there somewhat, individual effort strug-
gling up in a thousand free ways.

The individual freedom which we possess is
a great reason for individual exertion. How
large that freedom is, it needs but a slight
acquaintance with the past to estimate.
Through what ages have we not toiled to the
conviction that people should not be burnt
for their opinions. The lightest word about
dignities, the slightest claim to freedom of
thought or speech upon those matters which,
perhaps, angelic natures would hardly venture to pronounce upon, even the wayward
play of morbid imagination, were not un-
likely in former times to lead to signal pun-
ishments. A man might almost in his sleep
commit treason, or heresy, or witchcraft. The
most cautious, official-spoken man amongst
us, if carried back on a sudden to the
days of Henry the Eighth, would, at the end
of the first week, be pursued by a general
hue and cry from the authorities, civil and
ecclesiastical, for his high and heinous words

against King, Church, and State. While now, Alfred Tennyson justly describes our country as

> " The land, where girt with friends or foes,
> " A man may say the thing he will."

There is danger of our losing this freedom if we neglect the duties which it imposes. But I have resolved to avoid dwelling upon dangers, and would rather appeal to other motives. The triumph for a nation so individually free as ours, would be to show that the possible benefits of despotism belonged to it—that there should be paternal government without injurious control—that those things should ultimately be attained by the exertions of many which a despot can devise and execute at once, but which his successor may, with like facility, efface. Whereas what is gained for many by many, is not easily got back. It must be vast embankments indeed which could compel that sea to give up its conquests.

We have now gone through the principal
means by which social remedies may be effected : there comes the consideration within
what limits these means should be applied.
The subject of interference is a most difficult
one. We are greatly mistaken, however, if
we suppose that the difficulty is confined to
Government interference. Who does not
know of extreme mischief arising from over-
guidance in social relations as well as in
state affairs? The inherent difficulty with
respect to any interference, is a matter which
we have to get over in innumerable transactions throughout our lives. The way in
which, as before said, it appears to me it
should be met, is principally by enlightenment as to the purposes of interference.
Look at the causes which are so often found
to render interference mischievous. The governing power is anxious to exalt itself;
instead of giving life and energy, wishes
only to absorb them. Or it is bent upon
having some outward thing done, careless
of the principles on which it is done, or

of the mode and spirit of doing it. Hence, in public affairs, things may be carried which have only a show of goodness, but in reality are full of danger; and in private life, there arise formality, hypocrisy, and all kinds of surface actions. Or, again, the governing power is fond of much and minute interference, instead of, as Burke advises, employing means " few, unfrequent, and strong." There may also be another error, when from over-tenderness, or want of knowledge, the authority in question suffers those under its influence to lean on it, when they are strong enough to walk by themselves. All these errors are general ones, which require to be guarded against in the education of a child, as well as in the government of a state. All of them, too, have their root in an insufficient appreciation of the value of free effort. But when this is once attained, the interfering party will see that his efforts should mainly be enabling ones: that he may come as an ally to those engaged in a contest too great for their ability; but that he is not to weaken prowess by unneeded meddling. It may be said that this is vague. I am content to be vague upon a point where, I believe, the greatest thinkers will be very cautious of laying down precise rules. Look at what Burke says with regard to state interference—that it should confine itself to what is " truly and properly publick, to the " publick peace, to the publick safety, to the " publick order, to the publick prosperity." How large a scope do those words " publick " prosperity" afford. Besides, the transactions, in which we want to ascertain just limits for our interference, are so numerous, and so various, that they are not to be met but by an inconceivable multiplicity of rules. Such rules may embody much experience, but they seldom exhaust the subject which they treat of; and there is the danger of our suffering them to enslave, instead of merely to guide, our judgments. And then, on some critical occasion, when the exception, and not the rule, is in accordance with the principle on which the rule has been formed, we

may commit the greatest folly in keeping
to what we fancy the landmarks of sagacity and experience. Instead, therefore, of
laying down any abstract rules, I will only
observe that a primâ facie reluctance to all
interference is most reasonable, and perhaps
as necessary in the social world, as friction
is in the physical world, in order to prevent
every unguided impulse from having its full
mechanical effect: that, nevertheless, interference must often be resorted to: and that
the best security for acting wisely in any
particular case, is not to suffer ourselves to be
narrowly circumscribed by rules, but at the
same time to be very cautious of attempting
any mere present good, of getting notions of
our own rapidly carried into action, at the expense of that freedom and moral effort which
are the surest foundations of all progress.

We were considering, above, the claim
which our individual freedom makes on our
individual exertion for the good of others.
But this freedom must in some degree be

limited in order to produce its best results; and amongst them, to secure the greatest amount of such individual exertion. We know the restraint that must exist upon all, if all are to enjoy equal freedom. The freedom of one is not to be a terror to another. Law is based upon this obvious principle. But there are other circumstances also, in which individuals will find support and comfort in the general freedom being circumscribed by some interference on the part of the state or other bodies. Such a case occurs when the great majority of some class of private individuals would willingly submit to wise regulations for the general good, but cannot do so without great sacrifice, because of the selfish recusancy of some few amongst them. Here is a juncture at which the State might interfere to enable individuals to carry out their benevolent intentions. But one of the main reasons for some degree of interference from the State or other authorized bodies, in matters connected with our present subject, is that, otherwise, the responsibilities of individuals

would be left overwhelming. It is to be remembered by those who would restrain such
interference within the narrowest possible
bounds, that they by so much increase individual responsibility. Responsibility can,
happily, by no scheme, be made to vanish.
Wherever a signal evil exists, a duty lies somewhere to attack it. Suppose a district, for
instance, in which the state of mortality is
excessive, a mortality clearly traceable to the
want of sanitary regulations. In a despotic
government it may be enough to mention
this to the central body. In a free state,
where the duties of a citizen come in, more
is required from the individual; and if there
is no fit body of any kind to appeal to in
such a case, the burden lies upon all men
acquainted with the facts, to endeavour con-
jointly, or separately, to remove the evil.
While, on the one hand, we must beware of
introducing such interference, whether coming
from the State or other bodies, as might pa-
ralyse individual exertion, we must at the
same time remember that the weight to be

removed may be left overwhelmingly disproportionate to individual effort, or even to conjoint effort, if unauthorized, both of which
may thus be stiffened by despair into inac-
tion.

In the instance we have just been considering, we must not say that the people immediately interested in removing the evil will
do so themselves. It is part of the hypothesis that they will not. Ages have passed by,
and they have not. They do not know what
is evil. It has been observed that savages
are rarely civilized by efforts of their own.
A vessel from civilized parts comes and finds
them savages. A generation passes away.
Another vessel comes, how differently pro-
pelled, how differently constructed; manned
by sailors who have different costume, food,
ways of speech and habits from the former
ones; but they are able to recognize at once
the savages described by their forefathers.
These have not changed. The account of
them is as exact as if it were written yester-
day. In such a land, we must not look for

the germ of improvement amongst the miserable inhabitants themselves.   It must come
from without, brought thither by hopeful,
all-sympathizing enterprize.

CHAP. IV.

In what Spirit the Remedies are to

be effected.

WHENEVER the condition of the labouring people becomes a general
topic, some erroneous modes of discussing it
arise which deserve notice. In the first place,
there is a matter which, in all our friendly
efforts for the working classes, we must not
forget, and that is, to make these efforts with
kindliness to other classes. The abuse of
other people is an easy mode of showing our
own benevolence, more easy than profitable.
To alleviate the distress of the poor may be
no gain, if, in the process, we aggravate the
envies and jealousies which may be their
especial temptation. The spirit to be wished

for is sympathy; and that will not be produced by needless reproaches. Besides, it is
such foolish injustice to lay the blame of the
present state of things on any one class. It
is unpractical, unphilosophical, and incon-
sistent with history. If we must select any
class, do not let us turn to the wealthy,
whom, perhaps, we think of first. They have,
in no time that I am aware of, been the pre-
eminent rulers of the world. The thinkers
and writers, they are the governing class.
There is no doubt that the rich and great
have in most cases a large sphere of usefulness open to them; and they are fatally
blind, if they neglect it. That is, however,
rather a matter for them to think of, than
for those who are under them. And I feel
quite certain that the evils we are now, as a
nation, beginning to be sensitive to, are such
as may be more fairly attributed to the nation, in its collective capacity, than to any
one class, or even to any one generation. I
notice the error of the opposite opinion, believing it to be a signal hindrance to im-

provement. Let us not begin a great work with bitterness. I am not, however, for the slightest concealment of the truth, and can well understand the righteous indignation that will break out at witnessing the instances of careless cruelty to be seen daily. Still, this is not to be done by a systematic and undistinguishing attack upon any one class: if it requires a bold hand, it requires a just one also, under a reasonable restraint of humility. I suspect that those men, if any, who have a right to cast the first stone at their neighbour in this matter will be among the last persons to do so.

It is a grievous thing to see literature made a vehicle for encouraging the enmity of class to class. Yet this, unhappily, is not unfrequent now. Some great man summed up the nature of French novels by calling them the Literature of Despair: the kind of writing that I deprecate may be called the Literature of Envy. It would be extreme injustice to say that the writers themselves are actuated by an envious or malignant spirit.

It is often mere carelessness on their part, or ignorance of the subject, or a want of skill in representing what they do know. You would never imagine from their writings that some of the most self-denying persons, and of those who exert themselves most for the poor, are to be found amongst the rich and the well-born, including of course the great Employers of labour. Such writers like to throw their influence, as they might say, into the weaker scale. But that is not the proper way of looking at the matter. Their business is not to balance class against class, but to unite all classes into one harmonious whole. I think if they saw the ungenerous nature of their proceedings, that alone would stop them. They should recollect that literature may fawn upon the masses as well as on the aristocracy: and in these days the temptation is in the former direction. But what is most grievous in this kind of writing, is the mischief it may do to the working people themselves. If you have their true welfare at heart, you will not only

care for their being fed and clothed; but you
will be anxious not to encourage unreasonable
expectations in them, not to make them un-
grateful or greedy-minded. Above all, you
will be solicitous to preserve some self-reliance
in them. You will be careful not to let them
think that their condition can be wholly
changed without exertion of their own. You
would not desire to have it so changed. Once
elevate your ideal of what you wish to happen
amongst the labouring population; and you
will not easily admit anything in your writings that may injure their moral or their
mental character, even if you thought it might
hasten some physical benefit for them. That
is the way to make your genius most serviceable to mankind. Depend upon it, honest
and bold things require to be said to the
lower as well as to the higher classes; and
the former are in these times much less likely
to have such things addressed to them.

In the same way that we are fond of laying
the neglect, and the duty, of exertion upon

some class, even on our own, rather than on our especial selves, we are much given to look for something new which, in a magical manner, is to settle the whole difficulty. But when people look for a novelty of this kind, what do they mean? Some moral novelty? The Christian religion has been eighteen hundred years before the world, and have we exhausted the morality in that? Some political novelty? We are surely the nation, whose constitution, whatever may be said against it, has been most wrought and tempered by diverse thought and action. Some novelty in art or science? Where has man attained to a greater mastery over matter than in this iron-shearing country? The utmost that one age can be expected to do in the way of discovery is but little; and that little by few men. Let us sit down and make use of what we have. The stock out of which national welfare might be formed lies in huge, unworked-up masses before us. Social improvement depends upon general moral improvement. Moral improvement mostly comes, and at least is most safely looked for, not in the way of acquisition but of development. Now, as regards the conduct of the various classes of the state to each other, we do not want any new theory about it, but only to develop that kindly feeling which is already in the world between like and like, which makes a parent, for instance, so kind even to the faults of his children. We want that feeling carried over all the obstructions of imperfect sympathy which hedge it in now. This will be done by both classes knowing more of each other. One of the great reasons for the education of the people is, that even educating them a little enables rich and poor to understand each other better—in fact, to live more harmoniously together. If our sympathies were duly enlightened and enlarged, we should find that we did not need one doctrine for our conduct to friends, another for our conduct to dependents, and another for our conduct to neighbours. One spirit would suffice to guide us rightly in all these relations. The uninstructed man looking

around him on the universe, and seeing a
wonderful variety of appearances, is inclined
to imagine that there are numberless laws
and substances essentially different, little
knowing from how few of either the profusion of beauty in the world is formed. But
the creative energy of what we call Nature,
dealing with few substances, breaks out into
every form and colour of loveliness. Here,
we have the dainty floweret which I would
compare to the graceful kindnesses passing
among equals ; there, the rich corn-field like
the substantial benefits which the wise master-
worker confers on those around him ; here
again, the far-spreading oak which, with its
welcome depth of shade, may remind us of
the duties of protection and favour due from
the great to the humble ; and there, the
marriage of the vine to the elm, a similitude
for social and domestic affection. The kindnesses to which I have compared these various
products of Nature, are also of one spirit, and
may be worked out with few materials. Indeed, one man may in his life manifest them

all. No new discovery, no separate teaching, for each branch of this divine knowledge, is needed.

I do not say that there may not be physical discoveries, or legislative measures, which may greatly aid in improving the condition of the labouring classes. But, if we observe how new things come, in our own life for instance, or in the course of history, we shall find that they seldom come in the direction in which we are looking out for them. They fall behind us; and, while we are gazing about for the novelty, it has come down and has mingled with the crowd of old things, and we did not know it. Let us begin working on the old and obvious foundations, and we shall be most ready to make use of what new aid may come, if we do not find an almost inexhaustible novelty in what we deemed so commonplace. There is no way of burnishing up old truths like acting upon them.

You may rely upon it that it is one of the most unwholesome and unworkmanlike states of mind to be looking about for, and relying upon, some great change which is all of a sudden to put you into a position to do your duty in a signal manner. Duty is done upon truisms.

But let discoveries in morals or in physics have come; suppose any extent of political amelioration you please; and grant that the more outward evils have been conquered by combined effort. Let our drains flow like rivulets, and imagine that light and air permeate those dwellings which now moulder in a loathsome obscurity. Let the poor be cared for in their health, their amusements, their education, and their labour. Still the great work for an employer of labour remains for ever to be renewed; that which consists in the daily intercourse of life, in that perpetual exercise of care and kindness concerning those small things which, small as they may be, are nevertheless the chief part of men's lives. Perhaps the greatest possible amelioration of the human lot is to be found in the improvement of our notions of the duties of master to man. It were hard to say what could be named as an equivalent for even a slight improvement in that respect, seeing that there is no day in which millions upon millions of transactions do not come within its limits. If this relation were but a little improved, with what a different mind would the great mass of men go to their work in the morning, from the slave who toils amid rice fields in Georgia to the serf in Lithuanian forests. Nor would those far above the extremes of serfdom fail to reap a large part of the benefit. It cannot be argued that civilization renders men independent: it often fastens but more firmly the fetters of servitude —at least it binds them upon limbs more easy to be galled. Its tendency is to give harsh words the power of blows. Consider what a thing it is to be master. To have the kinglike privilege of addressing others first, to comment for ever on their conduct, while you are free from any reciprocal animadversion. Think what an immeasurable difference it must make, whether your subordinate feels that all he does is sure to be taken for the

best, that he will meet with continual graciousness, that he has a master who is good
lord and brother to him: or whether he lives
in constant doubt, timidity, and discomfort,
with a restless desire of escape ever upper-
most in his mind. I do not apply this only
to the ordinary relation of master and servant.
You sometimes see the most cruel use made
even of a slight social superiority, where the
cruelty is enhanced by the education and
other advantages of the suffering party. To
say nothing of Christianity, there is the
greatest want of chivalry in such proceedings,
in whatever rank they take place, whether
from masters to servants, employers to employed, or in those more delicately consti-
tuted relationships just alluded to. In all
our intercourse with those who have not a
full power of replying to us, instead of being
the less restrained on this account, which is
the case with most of us, the weakness on
the other side ought to be an irresistible claim
to gentleness on ours. The same applies
when what is naturally the weaker, being

guarded by social conventionalities on its side, is in reality the stronger, and is tempted into insolence, thus abusing the humanity of the world. But, let us turn from the abuse of power, and see what it is when wielded by discerning hands. It is like a healthful atmosphere to all within its boundaries. Other benefits come and go, but this is inhaled at every breath, and forms the life of the man who lives under it. It is a perpetual harmony to him, " songs without words," while he is at his work. One of the most striking instances we have had in modern times of this just temperament of a master was to be noted in Sir Walter Scott. The people dependent upon him were happier, I imagine, than you could have made them, if you had made them independent. If you could have distributed, as it were, Scott's worldly prosperity, you cannot easily conceive that it would have produced more good than when it fell full on. him, and was forthwith radiated to all around him. You may say that this was partly the result of genius. Be it so. Genius is, by

the definition of it, one of the highest gifts.
If, with humble means, we can produce some
of its effects, it is great gain. Without, however, wishing to depreciate the attaching influence of genius, we must, I think, attribute
much of this admirable bearing in Scott to an
essential kindliness of nature and a deep sense
of humanity. If he had possessed no peculiar
gifts of expression or imagination, and quietly
followed the vocation of his father, a writer
to the Signet, he would have been loved in
his office as he was on his estate; and old
clerks would have been Laidlaws and Tom
Purdies to him. Scott would under any circumstances have insisted on being loved: he
would have been " a good lord and brother"
to any man or set of men over whom he had
the least control. You cannot make out that
true graciousness of his to be a mere love of
feudal usages. It is the best thing that remains of him, better than all his writings, if,
indeed, it were not visible throughout them.

The duties of master to man are the more
important, because, however much the rela-

tion may vary in its outward form, it will not
be mapped down as in this or that latitude,
but remains as pervading as the air. We
may have brought down the word charity to
its most abject sense, considering what is
but the husk of it to be the innermost kernel.
Mere symbols of it may go on. In times,
when few things were further apart than
charity and papal sway, the popes still went
through the form of washing poor men's feet.
But that symbol has a wondrous significance
—the depth of service which is due from all
masters, the humble charity which should
ever accompany true lordship and dominion.

When considering in what spirit our remedies should be attempted, one of the most
important things to be urged is, that it should
be in a spirit of hopefulness.

In one of Dr. Arnold's letters there is the
following passage. " 'Too late,' however,
" are the words which I should be inclined
" to affix to every plan for reforming society
" in England; we are ingulfed, I believe, in-

" evitably, and must go down the cataract;
" although ourselves, i. e. you and I, may be
" in Hezekiah's case, and not live to see the
" catastrophe." Similar forebodings were
uttered on other occasions by this eminently
good man in the latter years of his life. I quote
the passage to show how deep must have been
the apprehension of danger and distress which
could so depress him; and, more especially,
for the purpose of protesting against any similar despondency which I fear to be very
prevalent in these times. It mainly arises, as
it seems to me, from a confusion between the
term of our own life and that of the state.
We see a cloud which overshadows our own
generation, and we exclaim that the heavens
and earth are coming together. How often,
in reading history, does a similar feeling occur to us. We think, how can the people
we are reading of revive after this whirlwind
of destruction! Imagine how much more
they themselves must have felt despondency.
A Northumbrian looking upon William the
Conqueror's devastations—a monk consi-

dering the state of things around him in the exterminating contest of Stephen and Matilda, or the wars of the Roses—the remaining one of a family swept off by some of those giant epidemics which desolated our towns in the fourteenth century—a member of the defeated party in the struggles of the Reformation, the Rebellion, or the Revolution—what would any such person have prophesied as to the fate of his country? How little would he have foreseen the present plethoric, steam-driving, world-conquering England! So with us. We too have evils, perhaps of as large dimension, though in some respects of a totally different character from those which our forefathers endured—and did not sink under. Nothing is to be shunned more than Despair. How profound is the wisdom which has placed Hope in the front rank of Christian virtues. For is it not the parent of endeavour? And in this particular matter, the improvement of our social condition, the more we examine it, the more we shall discover cause for hope. The evils

are so linked together that a shock given to
any one would electrify the whole mass of
evil. Take an instance. Suppose that those
who have the means bestir themselves to improve the houses of the poor. See what good
will flow from that. Physical suffering is di-
minished; but that is, perhaps, the least thing.
Cleanly and economical habits are formed;
domestic occupations are increased; more
persons live through the working period of
life; and a class is formed low down in the body
politic who are attached to something, for a
man who has the tenancy of a good house to
lose, is not altogether destitute. And under
what circumstances is all this done? By the
more influential classes taking a kindly concern in a matter in which all are deeply
interested. This is not the least part of the
good. Indeed, without it, all the rest, however excellent in itself, would lack its most
engaging features. Seeing then in one instance how much good may be done even
with slight efforts, we may determine to resist despondency. To yield to it, even but

a little, is to help in building up the trophy
for the other side.

Although we must not listen to despondency, we must not, on the other hand, attempt to conceal from ourselves that this subject, the "condition of England question" as
it has been called, is oppressively large; or
suppose that it can be dealt with otherwise
than by ever-growing vigour. At the present
moment public attention is unusually fixed
upon it. But this may be of brief duration.
The public soon becomes satiated with any
subject. Some foreign war, or political contest, may all at once turn its looks in far other
directions. But the social remedies that we
have been talking of, are not things to be fin-
ished by a single stroke. We cannot expect
to complete them just while the daylight of
public opinion is with us. The evil to be
struggled against is a thing entwined with
every fibre of the body politic. It is enough
to occupy the whole mind of the age; and
demands the best energies of the best minds.
It should be a " Thirty years' war" against

sloth and neglect.   It requires men who will
persevere through public favour or disfavour,
who can subdue their own fastidiousness, be
indifferent to ingratitude, tolerant of folly,
who can endure the extreme vexation of
seeing their most highly prized endeavours
thwarted by well intentioned friends, and
who are not dependent for reward upon those
things which are addressed to vanity or to
ambition.

After a long fit of distress which, for the
poorer classes, may almost be called a seven
years' famine, we are now apparently entering upon one of our periodic times of prosperity.   You hear of thousands of additional
"hands" being wanted, of new mills rising
up, and at last of a revival of the home
trade.   It is one of those "breathing spaces"
in which we can look back with less despondency, and forward with some delibera-
tion.   Each man's apprehensions for his own
fortunes need no longer absorb his whole
attention.   Yet one cannot observe all this

clashing and whizzing of machinery, this crowding on our quays, this contention of railway projects, and the general life and hum of renewed activity, without a profound fear and sadness lest such things should pass on, as their predecessors have passed, leaving only an increased bulk of unhandy materials to be dealt with. It is one of those periods upon which the historian, armed with all that wisdom which a knowledge of the result can furnish him, may thus dilate in measured sentences. " A time of nearly seven years " of steady distress had now elapsed ; nor " can it be said, that this distress had been " lightly regarded by thoughtful minds, or " that its salutary process had not com- " menced. The question of the condition of " the labouring classes had in a measure be- " come prominent. The Essayist moralized " about it after his fashion ; the lover of sta- " tistics arrayed his fearful lists of figures to " show its nature and extent; the writer of " fiction wove it into his tale ; the journalist " found it a topic not easily to be exhausted :

" old men shook their heads over it; and the
" young, to the astonishment of the world,
" began to talk of it as a matter of pressing
" interest to them. Now was the time when
" Great Britain might have looked into this
" question. But a return of prosperity, which
" we must almost call insidious, lulled atten-
" tion. Sickness and adversity are soon for-
" gotten. And this nation awoke as from a
" bad dream which it was by no means de-
" sirous of recalling in its daylight reminis-
" cences." My friends, let us not give an
opportunity to the historian to moralize upon
us in this manner. If we are employers of
labour, let us bethink ourselves that now is
the time for persuading our men to do something for themselves; now is the time for
getting improvements made in our town and
neighbourhood, the public being in a cheerful
mood; now, too, we can ourselves adventure
something for the good of those around us.
Do not let us be anxious to drain the cup of
prosperity to its last drop, holding it up so
that we see nothing but it. Let us carry our-

selves forward in imagination, and then look backward on what we are doing now. That is the way to master the present, for the best part of foresight is in the reflex. What matter is it how many thousands of pounds we make, compared to how we make them?

" Yes," some one will reply, " the imagi-
" nary historian deserves to be heard. This
" is the time for the nation to do something.
" Really a Government with a surplus should
" put all things to rights." Oh, these un-happy collective nouns, what have they not to answer for ! This word " nation," for instance : we substitute it instead of writing down some millions of names, a convenience not altogether to be despised. But yours, my friend, is there. The word nation is not an abstract idea ; but means an aggregate of human beings. No individual man is elimi-nated by this process of abbreviation. Your being one of a nation is to enrich you with duties, not to deprive you of them. But these large words often soothe us into obli-viousness. It puts one in mind of long alge-

braical operations in which the student has wholly lost sight of reality, and is driving on his symbols, quite unable to grasp their significance. This may be well enough for him, for eventually some result comes out which can be verified. But if we, in active life, play with general terms, we do not come to such distinct results, but only get into profound confusion, as it will be in this case, if we expect great things to happen from some combined effort in their corporate capacity of those who, as individuals, are looking on.

Before we leave off, let us look at the subject in its full scope. A large portion of our fellow countrymen are living, not in a passive state of distress, but in one which manufactures rapidly disease, and poverty, and crime. I think it has been shown that it is in the power of other classes to raise this condition. At any rate it is in their power to make the attempt. There is no occasion for waiting—each of us can do

something to-day in this matter. Now consider what would be the effect of success in
these endeavours. Let us not take the other
result as probable; or, even in hypothesis,
draw any picture that might make despondency plausible. Suppose, then, the success of
individual, or united efforts, in raising the
condition of the labouring classes. What an
undivided good it is. Has any man some
particular reform at heart, some especial
hopes for his race? Where can he look for
such a basis to rest upon as in the improved
condition of the largest layer of the people?
What a field it opens for science, literature,
and art. What freedom may it not give to
the highest ranges of thought.

I cannot think the destinies of our race
an unimproving matter of contemplation, and
that it savours of presumption, or of needless forelooking, to reflect on these things.
A notable portion of the great human family
utters every day a prayer in which the individual supplicant asks, not for himself alone,
even those blessings which he can individually
enjoy, but also, and first, implores those

general blessings which include the welfare of his own race at least.   What is the meaning of this, if we are to take no interest in the general welfare, or not, by every means in our power, to aid in it?

In the better order of men there is a desire for social improvement totally independent of all thought of personal gain. Bishop Butler saw in the fact, that there were persons who devoted themselves to a pursuit so remote from worldly ends as astronomy, a wonderful instance of the innate consciousness in man of his high origin and destiny.   But an earnest and unselfish love of social progress, is a far more satisfying sign that the impress of good is not altogether effaced, and that men are not wholly isolated by worldliness from the future and the past.

" Hence, in a season of calm weather,
    Though inland far we be,
Our souls have sight of that immortal sea
    Which brought us hither,
    Can in a moment travel thither,
And see the Children sport upon the shore,
And hear the mighty waters rolling evermore."

FINIS.

APPENDIX.

APPENDIX.

THE following table shows the progressive decrease in the sum of vitality in the three classes of the inhabitants of Preston. The calculations are founded on the ages at death for the six years ending June 30, 1843:—

	1. Gentry.	2. Tradesmen.	3. Operatives.
Born	100	100	100
Remaining at the end of 1st year	90·8	79·6	68·2
,, ,, 2nd year	87·6	73·5	57·5
,, ,, 5th year	82·4	61·8	44·6
,, ,, 10th year	81·1	56·6	38·8
,, ,, 20th year	76·3	51·6	31·5
,, ,, 30th year	72·3	45·9	25·2
,, ,, 40th year	63·4	37·5	20·4
,, ,, 50th year	56·	28·1	15·6
,, ,, 60th year	45·1	20·5	11·2
,, ,, 70th year	25·4	13.3	6·1
,, ,, 80th year	8·	4·5	2·1
,, ,, 90th year	1·3	·8	·2
,, ,, 100th year	. .	. .	·03
	Terminates in the 92nd year.	Terminates in the 96th year.	Terminates in the 103rd year.

Evidence of Rev. J. Clay. Health of Towns Report, page **174.**

The following table shows the progressive decrease in the vitality of the three classes from the age of 21 years:—

	Gentry, &c.	Tradesmen, &c.	Operatives.
21 years old	100	100	100
Remaining at 30 years old .	94·7	89·4	79·7
,, 40 years old .	83·2	73·2	63·7
,, 50 years old .	73·4	55·0	48·9
,, 60 years old .	59·1	40·4	34·6
,, 70 years old .	33·4	26·5	18·9
,, 80 years old .	10·8	9·6	7·1
,, 90 years old .	1·6	1·5	1·1
,, 100 years old .	. .	. .	0·6
	Terminates at 92 years.	Terminates at 96 years.	Terminates at 103 years.

Evidence of Rev. J. Clay. Health of Towns Report, page 175.

PROXIMATE ESTIMATE of Pecuniary and other SAVING from Sanitary Improvements in Preston.

1	2	3	4	5	6	7	8
Saving by one-third of the actual number of Deaths. The expense of each being estimated at 2l. 10s.	Saving in the excess of Births beyond 1 in 44 of the Population; the expense of each Birth being taken at 1l.	Saving in day's labour from sickness, estimating one-third of the cases out of the expense. 16,710 Cases.	Reduction by one-half of the existing expense of Widowhood and Orphanage, the amount taken from the actual expenditure.	Saving in the expense of Insurance, by keeping the water on night and day, so as to be in readiness at one minute's notice. Estimated on half the number of Houses at 6s. per House.	Saving of Productive Manure estimated at 10s. per head on the whole Population. All liquid and solid Manure and Street Sweepings being carried out of Town by the Sewers.	Saving in Washing, &c. consequent on the burning of Factory Smoke. Estimated at 1d. per head per week of the Population.	Saving of outside painting of Shops and Houses; estimating the cost per House at 25s. and the saving at one-fourth of the sum.
£. 1,240	£. 827	£. 7,047	£. 501	£. 15,000	£. 25,000	£. 10,450	£. 1,250

	£.	s.	d.
Total annual saving to the town	47,815	0	0
Total weekly saving to the town	919	10	4
Total annual saving to each house	4	15	7
Total weekly saving to each house	0	1	10
Total annual saving to each individual	0	19	1
Total weekly saving to each individual	0	0	4¼

Evidence of Rev. J. Clay. Health of Towns Report, page 197.

Proximate Estimate of Expenditure.

	Total Number of Houses.	A. Cost per House for Capital.	B. Rent per House.	C. Total Outlay.	D. Total Increased Rental required defraying by Annual Instalments of Principal and Interest of 20 Years for the House cleansing and Water Apparatus, and 30 Years for Sewers and Drains.
		£. s. d.	s. d.	£.	£. s. d.
1. In want of water	5,000	0 10 0	0 6	2,500	200 15 0
2. main sewer	10,000	0 5 0	0 2	2,500	162 12 6
secondary do.	7,919	2 9 6	2 6	19,599	1,274 18 9
3. house-drains	10,000	0 15 0	0 9	7,500	487 17 9
4. water closets	10,000	2 0 0	2 0	20,000	1,606 1 0
5. ventilation	10,000	0 15 0	0 9	7,500	602 4 6
6. street-sweeping	10,000	. . .	9 3	. . .	4,625 0 0

	£.	s.	d.
Total immediate expenditure of capital required for the improvement of the town	51,599	0	0
Total increased rental (including the annual expense of street-sweeping)	8,959	9	8
Immediate expenditure for each house	5	19	3
Total increased annual rent for each house	0	15	11
Total increased weekly rent for each house	0	0	3¾
Immediate expenditure per head of the population	1	3	9
Annual expenditure per head of the population	0	3	6¼
Weekly expenditure per head of the population	0	0	0¾ ¹⁴⁄₅₂

Evidence of Rev. J. Clay. Health of Towns Report, page 196.

DR. ARNOTT TO THE AUTHOR, ON THE SUBJECT OF VENTILATION.

Bedford Square, January, 1845.

MY DEAR SIR,

To aid the memory of persons inquiring about the means of preserving health, I have elsewhere endeavoured to mark clearly, that the four things, fit *air*, *temperature*, *aliment*, and *exercise*, are all that need to be secured, and the two things *violence* and *poisons* all that need to be avoided, by men of sound constitution, that they may enjoy uninterrupted health and long life;— and consequently that the causes of all other disease than the decay from age are to be looked for in errors committed in regard to these four necessaries, or in the direct influence of these two kinds of noxious agents. The tabular view on the opposite page, now to be examined, exhibits the subject to the eye.

In some moderately warm and uniform climates of the earth, such as the Azores or Western Isles in the Atlantic, the two first mentioned necessaries, viz. fit temperature and pure air, are so constantly present that the inhabitants no more think of them as necessaries to be laboured for than they think of the gravitation which holds their bodies to the earth as such a necessary. But in colder, or changing climates, to procure house-shelter, clothing, and fuel, for cold weather becomes a very considerable part of the necessary business of life. And where food is dear, that is to say, obtainable only as the reward of much labour, as is true in England, the amount

THE FOUR NECESSARIES.

In fit Kind and Degree.	In Deficiency.	In Excess.
1. AIR . . .	Suffocation . . Unchanged Air.	Excess of Oxygen.
2. TEMPERATURE	Cold (intense) .	Heat (intense.)
3. ALIMENT :— Food . .	Hunger . . .	Gluttony, or Surfeit.
Drink . .	Thirst	Swilling water.
4. EXERCISE :— Of the body	Inaction . . . or	Fatigue or Exhaustion.
Of the mind	Ennui . . . . Certain depressing passions, as fear, sorrow, &c.	Want of Sleep. Certain exciting passions, as anger, jealousy, &c.
Of the mixed social aptitudes.	Solitude . . .	Debauchery.

THE TWO NOXIOUS AGENTS.

1. VIOLENCE :—
   Wounds,—Fractures,—Burns, &c.—Lightning.

9. POISONS :—
   Animal, Mineral, Vegetable.

   Certain of these, such as *alcohol* in its various forms, opium, tobacco, &c. which in large quantities kill instantly, when they are taken in very moderate quantity can be borne with apparent impunity, and are sometimes classed as articles of sustenance, or they may be medicinal, but if taken beyond such moderation, they become to the majority of men destructive slow poisons.

   Contagions,—as of plague, small-pox, and measles.

   Malaria of marshes, thickets, and of filth.

of labour which individuals can perform with safety to their health, is often not sufficient to supply all the urgent wants.

Exposure to temperature lower than what suits the human constitution is so severely felt, that persons, even before fixed disease has arisen as a consequence, cannot remain indifferent to it; and how little soever some minds are disposed to reflect or speculate on such subjects, there are few who are not aware that all the diseases which in this and other climates are called winter diseases, as catarrhs, quinsies, pleurisies, croups, rheumatisms, &c. &c. are consequences of error in regard to temperature. But only persons whose attention has been specially directed to the subject become fully aware of the fatal influence of that want of fresh air which the closeness or otherwise faulty construction of dwellings occasions. The immediate effect is little felt, although the insidious enemy is unfailingly producing diseases perhaps more destructive even than those from cold, above enumerated. Impaired bodily and mental vigour, and the scrofulous constitution which renders persons more liable to many diseases and among these to consumption, the destroyer at present of about a sixth part of the inhabitants of Britain, may be cited as part of the effects.

In England, as yet, many singular and hurtful misconceptions prevail on the subjects of both warming and ventilating. The object of a little work which I published some time ago on these subjects, was to substitute for the misconceptions correct knowledge, and to describe some new and simple means of obtaining the objects sought. A considerable change, however, in common opinions and habits is not easily effected, and the co-operation of many labourers will be required to accomplish all that is here wanted. In a new edition of the book, now in preparation, I have attempted to convert some remarkable errors that have been committed in public situations into useful warnings or lessons for the future. It is but recently that even the members of our Houses of Parliament became aware that many of their body formerly had lost health, and even life, from want of a complete ventilation of the Houses, easy to be effected. And at present the havoc made in the crowded workrooms of milliners, tailors, printers, &c. and the injury done to young health in many schools, from similar want of knowledge, are most painful to contemplate. Without the requisite knowledge very expensive attempts are made with little or no benefit; with that knowledge, the desired ends may be completely attained at little cost.

The great error committed in regard to ventilation has been the want of an outlet in or near the cieling of rooms, for the air rendered impure in them by the breathing of inmates and the burning of candles, lamps, gas, &c. At present the only outlet of English rooms is the fire place or chimney opening near the floor. But all the impurities above referred to rise at once towards the cieling, because of the lessened specific gravity of air when heated, and there they would at once escape by a fit opening. Where there is no such opening, however, they become diffused in the upper air of the room, and can escape only slowly by diving under the chimney-piece as that air is changed. Thus the air of a room above the level of the fire-place, whenever there are people or lights in the room, must always be loaded, more or less, with impurity. The purest air of the room is that near the floor, being the last that entered, and the coolest, therefore and heaviest specifically; and with this the fire is fed, while the hotter impure air remains almost stagnant above, around the heads and mouths of the company. To remove the evil here referred to, I have shown, that even with an open fire, if the throat of the chimney be properly narrowed by a register flap, an opening made near the cieling into the chimney flue, with a valve in it to allow air from the room to enter the chimney, but allowing no smoke to come out—will serve very effectually; and that where there is no open fire the ventilation can, by the means described, be made still more complete.

The great error with respect to warming in rooms for many inmates has been to have all the heat radiating (none being given off by contact) from one focus or fire place, persons near to which consequently must receive too much, and those far from which will receive too little; while the supply of fresh air enters, cold, at a few openings chiefly, and pours dangerously on persons sitting near these. In common rooms, with open fires, the evils described may be lessened considerably by admitting fresh air through tubes or channels which open either near the fire, or all along the skirtings so that the fresh air is equally distributed over the room and mixed with the mass of air previously in it: but to have what is desirable, the air before distribution must be warmed by some of the simple means now known, as of warm channels in the brick work around the fire, or of the air being made to come into contact with the surface of properly regulated stoves, or tubes containing heated water. I have given detailed accounts of these means in the publication above referred to; and I have contrived and described various regulators applicable to stoves and to the furnaces of hot-water apparatus, which give complete command over the rate of combustion, and save nearly all the ordinary trouble of watching fires.

Then, to give complete efficiency to both the warming and ventilating apparatus described, I have had made a simple air-mover, or ventilating pump, which may be worked by a weight, like a kitchen jack, or by a treddle, like a spinning-wheel or turning-lathe; and which, in all states of wind and of temperature, will deliver by measure any quantity of air into or out of any inclosed space.

The means of ventilating and of warming now referred to, may in different cases be adopted in part or in whole. In the dwellings of the poor of cities, where the same room serves for all purposes,—working at a trade, sleeping, cooking, and is never unoccupied, a brick taken out of the wall, from near the cieling, over the fire-place, so as to leave there an opening into the chimney-flue, removes great part of the evil; and if a simple chimney-valve, which I have described, allowing air freely to enter the chimney, but no smoke to return, be added, and there be an additional opening made in some convenient part of the wall or window to admit and dis-tribute fresh air, where air enough cannot enter by the crevices and joints about the door and window, the arrangement might be deemed for such places complete. Even in a milliner's or tailor's crowded work room a larger opening of this kind into the chimney, with its balanced valve, and with a branching tube having in-verted funnel mouths over the gas lamps, or other lights, and conveying all the burned air to the valved opening*

* The author of this book has tried one of these " valved open-ings" recommended by Dr. Arnott, and has found it answer very well.

in the chimney, is so great an improvement on present practice, that many would deem it perfection. To this, however, may be added, at little cost, an opening for admitting, and channels behind the skirting for distributing, the fresh air; and to make the thing really complete, there must be also the means, by a stove or by hot water pipes, of warming the air before its distribution; and there must be the ventilating pump to inject and measure air when such action may be required. During the winter, in many cases the chimney draught would be sufficient to produce the desired currents of air without the pump.

All the means here spoken of have already been and are in satisfactory operation in various places. The chimney-valves have been made by Mr. Slater, gas-fitter, 23, Denmark Street, Soho, and Mr. Edwards, 20, Poland Street, Oxford Street. The pump by Mr. Bowles, 58, Great Coram Street, and Mr. Williams, 25, Upper Cleveland Street. The stoves by Mr. Edwards, Poland Street, Messrs. Bramah and Co. Piccadilly, Messrs. Bailey, Holborn, and others.

I am, my dear sir,

yours very truly,

N. ARNOTT.

CHARLES WHITTINGHAM, CHISWICK.